Rome Rising

by Fred DeRuvo

Rome Rising

Copyright © 2014 by Fred DeRuvo, for Study-Grow-Know

All rights reserved. Written permission must be secured from the publisher to use or reproduce any part of this book, except brief quotations in critical reviews or articles.

Published in Scotts Valley, California, by Study-Grow-Know
www.studygrowknow.com • www.studygrowknowblog.com

All Scripture, unless otherwise noted, is from the NASB. "Scripture quotations taken from the New American Standard Bible®, Copyright © 1960, 1962, 1963, 1968, 1971, 1972, 1973, 1975, 1977, 1995 by The Lockman Foundation. Used by permission." (www.Lockman.org)

Some original cartoons/images were created with ToonDoo, with copyright retained by Fred DeRuvo. For more information: http://www.toondoo.com/

Unless otherwise noted, all Figure illustrations used in this book were created by the author and protected under copyright laws, © 2014.

Cover design by Fred DeRuvo

Cover image: © CURAphotography - Fotolia.com

Edited by: Hannah Brady

Library of Congress Cataloging-in-Publication Data

DeRuvo, Fred, 1957 –

ISBN 0988183358
EAN-13 978-0-9881833-5-3

1. Religion – Christian Theology - Eschatology

Contents

Foreword:	5
Chapter 1: First Things First	8
Chapter 2: Understanding the Roman Empire	13
Chapter 3: Secret Societies	19
Chapter 4: Daniel 2: Before Rome Began	35
Chapter 5: Do Empires Really Die?	46
Chapter 6: All the Same Geography	60
Chapter 7: More About the Roman Empire	74
Chapter 8: Ottoman Turkish Rule	84
Chapter 9: Daniel 2 Revisited	94
Chapter 10: Daniel 7	103
Chapter 11: Revelation 13, Part 1	118
Chapter 12: Revelation 13, Part 2	138
Chapter 13: Character of the Fourth Empire	144
Chapter 14: EU Land & Sovereignty Grab	152
Chapter 15: Genocide is Part of the Plan	165
Chapter 16: The Elite's Future Dreams	178
Chapter 17: The Elite's Future Demise	189
Chapter 18: Can Your Belief System Save You?	195
Resources for Your Library	207

Then I saw a beast coming up out of the sea, having ten horns and seven heads, and on his horns were ten diadems, and on his heads were blasphemous names. And the beast which I saw was like a leopard, and his feet were like those of a bear, and his mouth like the mouth of a lion. And the dragon gave him his power and his throne and great authority.

– Revelation 13:1-2

FOREWORD

In today's day and age, it is extremely important that Christians understand several things about why we are here in this world. First, once we become Christians, God leaves us here in order to become evangelists for Him. Second, the devil will do whatever it takes to move us from that path.

I believe it is way too easy for the enemy of our souls to sidetrack Christians from the job at hand. That job is the Great Commission.

It's easy for him to sidetrack us because of several things:

1. Today's Christian does not know God's Word like it should be known
2. Christians often fail to realize that there is a deeply spiritual connection between knowing His Word and growing in Him
3. Christians do not know how to refute the errors of today's society, especially when it comes to Islam
4. Too many Christians have fallen under the spell of emotional virtue, as opposed to being guided by absolute truth

Do you see yourself in any of the above scenarios? If so, then it's not too late to do something about it. The solution comes about by adjusting our goals so that they fall in line with God's. It also comes about by endeavoring to get into His Word more than ever.

How can an automobile be expected to drive in a straight line if the steering mechanism is not connected properly to the wheel base? How can a person expect him or herself to make decisions based on God's absolute truth if he or she is too often taken in by emotion?

How can a person adequately explain the Gospel to people if he cannot adequately understand it himself? Understanding what Christianity consists of is the beginning of being able to explain it to others.

The person who has only a general idea of what the Bible says about certain things will never be able to provide responses to people who either doubt or cast aspersions on God's Word.

While this book will examine the various Gentile empires listed in Daniel 2 primarily and how those empires lead up to the physical return of Jesus in which He will set up His Millennial Kingdom, we should never lose sight of the fact that we are here to spread the Gospel. We cannot allow ourselves to become distracted by Eschatology (study of last days) so that it is just a study. We must use it for our advantage. If knowing about the end times does not light a fire to go out and win souls, you are studying it for the wrong purposes.

We need to know God's plans and purposes primarily because He reveals them to us in His Word. It is very helpful to understand what God is doing (or allowing) in this world. That said, we must remain true to our calling.

In order to learn what God is doing, we will look at Daniel 2 (and 7) to see how God has lined things up to the very day that Jesus returns to this earth in judgment. We will also reference secular history and biblical passages other than Daniel 2. We will trace a path from the first of these empires (that began the Times of the Gentiles), starting with the Babylonian Empire through to the Roman Empire. Beyond this, we will discuss the final empire that is highlighted in Daniel 2, what many have called the Revised Roman Empire.

If Rome essentially died off, what, if anything, replaced it? If the old Roman Empire is slated to rise again, how is that understood from Scripture? Moreover, if the Bible teaches that it will rise again, what form will it take and in what way might we see it come to fruition?

In studying about these historical and ancient empires, we'll learn how God worked through the leaders/rulers of old. In some cases, He called these rulers by name long before they were even born.

While God uses leaders to accomplish His goals, the best people that God uses for the purposes of evangelism are not the Nebuchadnezzars, the Alexanders, the Cyruses or others like them. To be sure, God raises these individuals up for His purposes as well, but the truth of the matter is that those purposes normally have to do with the nation of Israel and bringing this world to the point where it will ultimately recognize the King of kings and Lord of lords.

In the meantime, God has chosen to use the Peters, the Pauls, the Stephens and others of the Bible. He's also chosen to use you (if you're an authentic Christian) and me to spread the truth of His Gospel to those who are perishing.

Nebuchadnezzar wasn't interested in that and neither was Alexander the Great. Yet God employed their talents in order to shape society for His purposes. He is still doing that, by the way: using people we may see as completely godless to bring His agenda to fruition.

It is my hope that as you read this book, you will be directed time and time again back to His Word and that you will eventually and ultimately understand that out of all the things you might accomplish in this life, there is no higher calling than participating in one that brings truth and salvation to the lost. That is why we are here. Everything else will fall into place, but let our hearts be moved to be evangelists for Him.

Fred DeRuvo, May 2014

Chapter 1
First Things First

It is very important to understand a number of things before getting too deeply into this book. As noted in the Foreword, the Gospel message is the most important truth that any Christian can share with another human being. Life can be bad or good and things from both categories happen to all people. No one is immune.

However, this life is not eternity, though it certainly leads to it. Where we place our faith (in Self or Christ) will determine where we spend eternity once we leave this life and enter the eternal state. Because of that, preaching the Gospel both in and out of seasons to all people is the most important work we can ever involve ourselves in.

When I say preaching the Gospel, I'm talking about words, yes, but I'm also talking about our actions.

The trouble with many today is that the Gospel truth has taken a back seat to other things. The Emergent Church with its watered-down message of God loving everyone stops there. The Emergent Church rarely, if ever, goes into detail about why people are perishing in the first place.

The purpose of the Emergent Church is to make sinners feel good about their lives. The goal is to make people believe that God acquiesces to us. He *has* stooped, of course, but only in so far as Jesus lived a sinless life, allowing Him to become the perfect propitiation for our sin. The need for each individual is to still receive that one and only salvation that is offered individually. It's not group therapy. Salvation is entering into a one-on-one relationship with Jesus Christ, the second Person of the Trinity.

Without doubt, the Gospel message must be preached to people and it must be preached repeatedly so that people have every chance to hear it and respond to it. Did you become a Christian the very first time you heard the Gospel? It probably required several hearings before you made a decision.

Too many today believe there are more important things to do than present the Gospel *first*. We must clothe the naked, feed the hungry, and become immersed in the process of social activism before we can actually present the truth of the Gospel. That's wrong. Desperately wrong.

There is no reason we cannot do both things – take care of the physical needs of a person (as we are able to do so) while presenting the Gospel to them. This can happen at the same time, but too many believe it is enough to simply do things for people. Do we need to be reminded of Peter's response to the beggar in Acts 3:6? There, he said, *"I do not possess silver and gold, but what I do have I give to you: In the name of Jesus Christ the Nazarene—walk!"*

Peter gave what he had and what he had was eternal truth, not material items that might even have helped feed the man. Peter gave something of eternal value even though he could not help the man physically at that point.

Jesus often fed the hungry. He healed the sick and infirm. He also always preached the truth about Himself and the Kingdom of Heaven wherever He went. He never simply gave people food without pointing them to the truth.

Too often in society today, we do not follow His example. That needs to change because time is of the essence and eternity is fast approaching for all people.

One thing we need to realize when it comes to presenting the Gospel message: It can't be done with our power and our might. It is done by God's Spirit. He is the One who empowers us to preach the Gospel and live a life that brings Him glory. Our words may seem weak and feeble, but God takes the truth we speak and uses it for His glory.

We can talk to people until we are blue in the face. We can create a warehouse of stockpiled food that will cause the hungry to have full stomachs. We can give out enough clothing so that no one goes unclothed again.

We can minister to people's medical needs and much more. But if we do not minister to their spiritual side, we haven't done anything with lasting eternal value. Wood, hay, and stubble is what we've created.

We need to get our priorities straight and stop fooling around, wasting God's time and ours. If we are not willing to tell people about the amazing grace of our Savior, we have no business calling ourselves Christian.

Some of the things that are going to be discussed in this book may cause readers to wonder why those subjects have been included. They are here for a reason, and hopefully those reasons will become clear as the reader continues to read.

In order to understand just how important the preaching of the Gospel is, we must come to understand what is going on in our world and how late the hour is for all of us. It is truly important that we grasp what the enemy is attempting to accomplish throughout this world. Once we do, we will have a better understanding of just how important and powerful God's message of truth is for the world to hear.

We are up against Satan but we are certainly not alone in our struggles. God is with us and empowers us for the fight. Our job is to depend upon Him for strength, wisdom, and discernment.

We also know from Scripture that Satan has already been beaten and simply awaits his predetermined appointment with the Lake of Fire. Until then, he is free to roam the earth and create havoc by bringing his goals and ambitions to fruition.

Of course, all of what Satan accomplishes is allowed to occur only because God allows it. He does so because the end result will be that God Himself is glorified. Because God loves us as much as He does, He has not left us without clues and even knowledge as to Satan's intentions and how he plans to brings those intentions to reality. That is why we have God's Word, because it is really a book that supersedes time itself.

In some ways, where prophecy is concerned, the Bible is a book that opens the doors to the future, and all of it was written in the past. Whether the human author was Daniel, Ezekiel, Zechariah, Joel, Paul, John, or Jesus, the implication that God's Word speaks about the future is not only amazing but incredible when considering the accuracy bound within each page of the biblical record.

In order to better understand exactly what we are up against, we need to take time to look back in history to know what the Bible reveals to us as far as the empires that have come (and are to still come). Gaining a good picture of what we see in Scripture will help us to know how Satan is working today.

Knowing this will also help keep us from being deflected from the main point. We will not get lost in useless arguments that do nothing to move the conversation forward. Like Jesus, we will present facts and let the chips fall where they will. God will use those facts to either open another person's eyes or not.

Chapter 2
Understanding the Roman Empire

For this book, it will be very important to understand some history, especially with respect to the Roman Empire. Without this understanding, we will miss the facts completely. We need to understand not only how the Roman Empire developed, but how it *fell*. Did it simply crumble overnight? Was its demise long in coming?

What we will learn is that the Roman Empire began its decline not long after AD 70 when Roman armies surrounded and destroyed Jerusalem. The Jewish Temple that stood during Jesus' day was also destroyed at this same time. Judgment that fell on the Roman Empire came in degrees, over hundreds of years.

Like any subject, there is certainly some disagreement among historians regarding when the Roman Empire officially ended. We will look at things as clearly as possible to determine what appears to be the most appropriate and logical time for the final demise of Rome. Many historians – like author Chris Wickham (*The Inheritance of Rome*) – argue that though the Roman Empire proper may have passed into death or obscurity, the legacy it left was adopted and incorporated into numerous cultures throughout Europe.

We will also delve into several areas of Scripture that will help us unlock things as related to the final beast (Daniel 2), which leads directly to what is often referred to by commentators as the Revised Roman Empire. Have your Bibles ready to view passages in Daniel, Revelation, and other areas of Scripture.

The Roman Empire had its beginnings as far back as 753 BC, if one goes by the somewhat mythical exploits of brothers Romulus and Remus. However, the reign of Romulus until 717 BC is considered to be the actual foundation of Rome itself. He was the first of seven legendary kings from which the Roman Empire eventually grew.[1]

Of course, this only references the *founding* of Rome and its early kings. How it grew into the great Roman Empire is another thing, eventually incorporating much of the geographical area conquered by Alexander the Great during his reign as the Grecian Empire.

Alexander's conquest of the Medo-Persian Empire began in approximately 334 BC. He succeeded to his father's throne after his father's death in 336 BC and continued his military campaign to expand the existing empire. Alexander was only twenty years of age at this point in time.

---

[1] http://en.wikipedia.org/wiki/King_of_Rome#Kings_of_Rome_.28753.E2.80.93509_BC.29

One of the most successful rulers of ancient times, Alexander's military prowess extended the empire of his father until Alexander's death at the age of 32 in 323 BC. At this point, because Alexander had no legitimate heir (a son was not born until *after* his death, by his mistress), his empire was then divided among four of his generals, with each general overseeing a geographical area of the Grecian Empire. These smaller groupings still made up the Grecian or Hellenistic Empire Alexander had created. They break down by general and geography as follows:

- Ptolemy
    - Egypt
    - Palestine
    - Arabia Petrea
- Seleucus
    - Syria
    - Babylonia
    - India
- Cassander
    - Macedonia
    - Greece
- Lysimachus
    - Thrace
    - Bithynia

After Alexander died, his four generals took over the rule of the Grecian Empire. Understandably, that empire began to wane in power. The Romans existed at this time as well, but remember, they were essentially a people centered in the city of Rome, Italy.

As time progressed, these Romans began to expand their area of rule through conflicts with neighboring peoples and also began to introduce their own form of technology, like the aqueduct. These technological marvels, along with their strength and sheer fearlessness,

Rome Rising

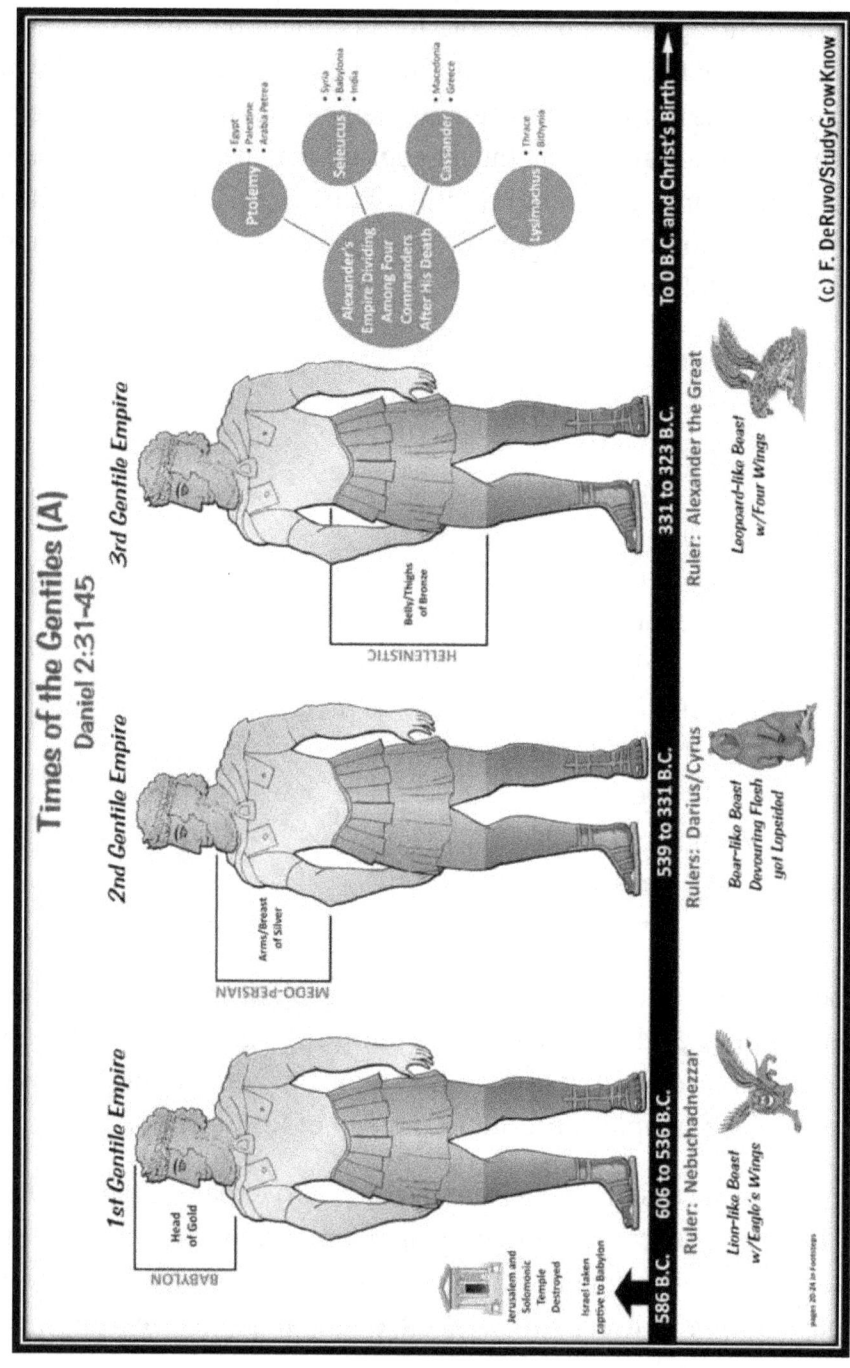

helped Rome become the greatest empire that has since existed in the world.

Roman history is filled with victories and defeats, but mainly defeats in the beginning. In 321 BC, the Romans were defeated by the Samnites. It was not until 295 BC that the Romans finally defeated the Samnites at Sentium.

In 275 BC, the Romans defeated King Pyrrhus of Epirus. Beyond this, the First Punic War (between Carthage in Northern Africa and Rome) occurred from 264 to 241 BC. It was during this time (260) that Rome built its first fleet of military ships. In 259, it gained the victory over Mylae at sea.

For the next several years, as Romans tried to expand their territory, there were numerous defeats (defeated at Africa, 265-255; defeated again at Drapana in 249), but they kept pushing onward. In 241 BC, Rome experienced victory off the Aegates Islands and claimed Sicily as their first province.

It was during this period of time that it appears Rome got her legs, so to speak, and began racking up victory after victory. Sardinia and Corsica were annexed in 238 BC. Yet the defeats occurred as well by the hand of Hannibal (Carthage) and others.

Though there were victories and defeats, power eventually shifted to Romans. By 168 BC, Macedonia became a Roman dependency.

Alongside this event, there was also a revolt against Antiochus Epiphanes IV, who had desecrated the Jewish Temple in Jerusalem. Jesus references this event as the "abomination that desolates" in Matthew 24, the Olivet Discourse, using it to point to the end of this age. More on this later.

The Third Punic War (northern Tunisia) occurred between 149 and 146 BC, with that part of Africa becoming a Roman province. By the time Jesus was born into humanity, Rome had become a very large empire indeed.

At the time of Jesus, Rome was feared throughout the known world. To be a soldier in the Roman army meant great power and respect. The average person feared Roman soldiers greatly and rightly so. These men were trained warriors. Their sole job was to be ready at a moment's notice to kill or be killed. They were not afraid of death and considered dying in the heat of battle the most honorable way a man could die.

Because the Roman Empire was so feared and respected due to its awesome power and prestige, people often paid a great deal of money just to become a citizen of Rome when not born there. This was a badge of honor, and privileges awarded the average citizen of Rome far exceeded the rights and privileges of those who were simply part of the empire, but not born in Rome.

Aside from all this, we all know that the Roman Empire ceased to exist as the Roman Empire at some point in history. It began and it ended, but when did it actually end?

Before we deal with that question, we will deal with the fact of secret societies dating back to antiquity. What has been the ultimate goal or purpose of these societies? Have they aimed to help or harm? Were they part of Rome's rise as the fourth empire of Daniel 2?

Following that chapter, we will open up God's Word to determine what we can know (if anything) about the Roman Empire. Does God say anything about it? We shall see.

Chapter 3
Secret Societies

Most people don't like to deal with things that are considered to be in the realm of "conspiracy theories," at least publicly. It immediately calls to mind people who wear tin hats, talk about alien abductions, or worse. The fact that many things discussed in that realm have not been proven simply makes it that much easier to deny.

People feel funny talking about these things, though many people believe to some extent that what we call conspiracy theories often have at least a kernel of truth in them. In my mind, there is a great deal of truth in at least some of these theories. The pieces fit together too easily to simply be relegated to coincidence.

We've also learned over time that at least some of the things people ridicule as being fodder for conspiracies or lunatic fringe-type thinking end up being true. Such was the case when Sarah Palin predicted in 2008 that due to Obama's weak foreign policy, one day Putin would attack Ukraine.[2]

Because of that comment, the world roared with laughter. Saturday Night Live (SNL) had a field day featuring skits with SNL alum Tina Fey impersonating Palin with the memorable line, "*I can see Russia from my house.*" Oh, it was good times, wasn't it? The idea of Putin invading Ukraine was such a fantasy from a "right-winger" that no one could believe it and there was nothing left to do except ridicule it and Palin unmercifully.

Of course, segue to April 2014 and the world appears to still be holding its collective breath wondering what the actual outcome will be with Ukraine, Crimea, Putin, and the EU. No one's laughing now, but neither is the left admitting they were wrong and Palin was correct. That's too much to expect.

This is the way things go in the world and it has never been truer than when dealing with conspiracies. Certainly, secret societies fall into that category because even though we have testimony, books, and articles from people who say they are in the know because they allegedly held certain positions with the government, knew people in secret societies, and/or appear to have insider knowledge from their own sources, it still boils down to what people are willing to believe. Nonetheless, we'll get into that forbidden area and I'll leave you to make your own decisions about secret societies and whether or not they rule the world from the shadows (insert dramatic music).

---

[2] http://www.breitbart.com/Big-Peace/2014/02/28/Flashback-Palin-Mocked-in-2008-for-Warning-Putin-May-Invade-Ukraine-if-Obama-Elected-President (4/10/2014)

There are many, *many* sources we could go to for information related to secret societies, and while we cannot refer to all of them, I'm actually going to start with Scripture. Aside from that, two individuals whom I believe to be the most credible are Daniel Estulin and Dr. John Coleman.

While I firmly believe so-called secret societies exist (and so should you since they do), the difference of opinion comes into play when people disagree about the *purposes* and *goals* of those secret societies. For instance, to most people, the Masons are a group of men who gather for benevolent purposes to help better humanity.

For others, the Masons are much darker than that, with truly ulterior motives, ultimately wanting to rule the world with people from other secret societies. However, the average Mason is not aware of the inner workings of that group and probably never will be. The only reason we know of them is due to people who were fairly high up in the organization, left, and lived to tell about it.

Nonetheless, secret societies did not start with the Masons or any modern-day group really. They began long ago.

In Genesis 10 we are introduced to a man named Nimrod who we learn was already a ruler of sorts. Here is what we learn from Genesis 10:8-9:

> *Now Cush became the father of Nimrod; he became a mighty one on the earth. He was a mighty hunter before the Lord; therefore it is said, "Like Nimrod a mighty hunter before the Lord."*

Of course, the next chapter – Genesis 11 – deals with the Tower of Babel where, after Nimrod had gathered everyone to himself, he led the people in building a tower that was to reach the heavens. We don't know why he wanted this done, but it likely had something to do with

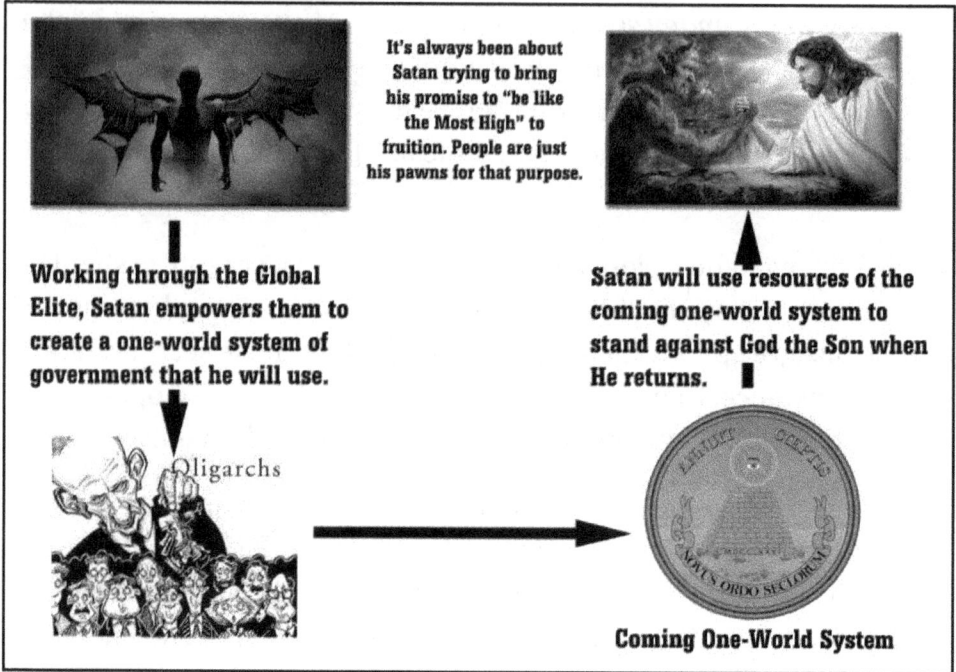

worshiping gods. Babylon – which ultimately came from that same geographical area – is known for its mystery religions.

We can honestly say that though God Himself went down and confounded the languages of the people so that they broke off into groups and went to different areas of the world, the mystery religions followed the people. The pursuit or even the worship of knowledge remained with humanity from that point onward. It began, of course, in the Garden of Eden when the serpent offered a way to Eve that would allow her to gain more knowledge.

I firmly believe that from the time of the fall, Satan has been working very hard to create a one-world system of government in order that he might rule this world himself through his spiritual son, the coming Antichrist. That seems obvious to me as I read Scripture and see what has been taking place in society. But it's not just ruling he's after. It's becoming "like the Most High" (cf. Isaiah 14) that drives him. He yearns to fulfill his promise.

Satan first tried to gain control of the entire earth and the people on it at the Tower of Babel. He only failed because God forced people into groups based on a common language.

Since that time, Satan has been rebuilding what he lost and it appears that God is allowing it this time, though it has taken several-thousand-plus years to get where it is today. Though not yet complete, it seems as though things are drawing to their conclusion.

What is important for people to realize is that what has been taking place and continues to occur in society is the result of Satan (a Hebraic title, not a name) promising to make himself equal with God. He did this in Isaiah 14:13-14.

> *I will ascend to heaven;*
> *I will raise my throne above the stars of God,*
> *And I will sit on the mount of assembly*
> *In the recesses of the north.*
> *"I will ascend above the heights of the clouds;*
> *I will make myself like the Most High."*

The last sentence in the above quote tells us what we need to know about Satan's aspirations. Of course, God's reply is immediate and negating. Not only would Satan not achieve his goals, but he would actually be thrown into hell itself (cf. Isaiah 14:15). This is his true and ultimate end, but God has allowed Satan to do what he can to bring his promises to fruition.

This is also why secret socities are so secret. They promise a wealth of secret gnosis (knowledge) to those who submit to and give up everything to worship the being they call Lucifer. To them, he is the true "light bearer" who came to humanity offering true knowledge designed to make life better for every individual.

There are many societies from antiquity that have worked to elevate Satan (aka Lucifer) to the level of godhood and by doing so have done what they can to alter the course of humanity to their benefit. In that way, all of these secret societies are connected due to their common goal for the world.

One of the oldest societies is known as the Brotherhood of the Snake. *"OF ALL THE animals revered in ancient human societies, none were as prominent or as important as the snake. The snake was the logo of a group which had become very influential in early human societies of both Hemispheres. That group was a disciplined Brotherhood dedicated to the dissemination of spiritual knowledge and the attainment of spiritual freedom"*[3]

There have been many secret societies, and in the end, the purpose is the same for each. It is to bring about a New World Order in which those who have done well and gained the secret knowledge will rule the rest of the world's population who have not.

Religion has always been used as a tool to control the masses. People yearn for secret knowledge that they believe will make them wiser and more gifted than others. They want to be in the know. They want to know things that others don't. It's like when someone confides in you. It makes you feel important to know one of their secrets, doesn't it? It's the same way on a grander scale with secret societies. Because this is one of the foundational aspects of all secret societies, this need for such a level of secrecy in and of itself should be enough to warn the average person that something is amiss.

Many of the mysteries that came into being and became part of the regular practices of people seeking to be illumined can be traced back to the mystery religions of Babylon. Prior to the Flood, the forbidden knowledge that came from fallen angels to humanity is very likely the driving force that caused all humanity to become corrupted. God destroyed most to save but a few (Noah and family).

---

[3] http://www.bibliotecapleyades.net/vida_alien/godseden/godseden03.htm
#Brotherhood of the Snake (4/15/2014)

However, it was the ancient civilization of Eygpt that incorporated much of the gnosis (or knowledge) gained from these mysteries into the public face of Egypt's religions. Though Egypt was not the first major civilization, it was first in many things, much of it based firmly on its worship of satanic deities.

What becomes very clear about these secret societies is what they all believe. Obviously, they want/need to further their own ends, not what's best for all of society. Remember, these people believe that they and they alone were put here to rule the rest of us. We need to keep that in mind. This is clearly what many of today's oligarchs or Global Elite believe.

David Rockefeller is probably one of the most well-known globalists in America. He has his fingers in everything. In his book – *Memoirs* – he even admits his ulterior motives for doing what he does.

> *For more than a century ideological extremists at either end of the political spectrum have seized upon well-publicized incidents such as my encounter with Castro to attack the Rockefeller family for the inordinate influence they claim we wield over American political and economic institutions. Some even believe we are part of a secret cabal working against the best interests of the United States, chracterizing my family and me as "internationalist"' and of conspiring with others around the world to build a more integrated global political and economic structure – one world, if you will. If that's the charge, I stand guilty, and I am proud of it.*[4]

In his arrogance, Rockefeller essentially admitted to working against the interests of the United States. That is treason, yet nothing happened to him because of his stature throughout the world.

---

[4] David Rockefeller, *Memoirs* (2002), p. 405

It's not as if Rockefeller made only that statement and left it there. The entire chapter I've just quoted from – "Proud Internationalist" – is replete with comments and statements supporting his main contention that he works for himself and other globalists toward a one-word system. My suggestion would be for you to buy his book and read it for yourself.

Rockefeller has been and/or is part of the Council on Foreign Relations (CFR) and the Trilateral Commission (which he created with the blessing of the Bilderberger group), as well as other agencies and groups. The real purpose of these groups has come to light due to the work of people like Daniel Estulin (at great risk to himself) and the sources they say they have within the Bilderbergers, people who have gotten fed up with the treaonous goals of said group and want to do what's right, but cannot leave for fear of their own or their family's lives.

Ultimately, though, the beliefs of these secret cabals are simple, yet they would cause most in the world to rebel if they were known. This is exactly why they remain secret societies. It is also exactly why so much of the information that people like Estulin have gained remains unbelievable to most. People simply cannot believe that groups like the Global Elite exist who have been directing societies throughout the world toward the goal of a one-world system. That appears to be the case though.

- They are working toward absolute control of the planet via control of
    - Wealth
    - Natural resources
    - People
- Their final goal is to convert the entire world into a Luciferian totalitarian socialist state

- They will eliminate anyone who does not agree with their program

If all this is true, then that is what we are working against. No wonder it is such an uphill battle, because while these are Satan's aspirations, God is certainly allowing it for His purposes. His purposes ultimately mean that in the end, He will be glorified in His absolute and unquestionable defeat of Satan.

When that happens, there will be no doubt in all the universe that God and only God is the true God. Satan is but a very poor and paltry imitator, one who pretends to be an angel of light but is evil through and through. Yet it is Satan who empowers humans to do his bidding, to make his goals a reality. This supernatural strength, fervor, and energy is the guiding factor in lives of people like David Rockefeller.

Men who have spent their entire adult lives as Freemasons have managed to get into every branch of government, including the Oval Office. Many to most presidents have been or are Freemasons. Beyond this, many of them are also members of the Knights of Malta, another secret society.

Again, all of these groups (at the top level) have one goal in mind: the complete dominance and rule of the entire world. Certainly not all Masons are aware of the deception. Only a few are brought into the real inner circle of Freemasonry. The rest never have an inkling about the real truth that lives in the shadows. They are merely the public face of the Masons, the buffer, if you will.

I quote William Cooper from his book *Behold a Pale Horse* only because it is so well known. However, there have been numerous people who have come forward to debunk much of what Cooper has stated to be fact. They also denigrate his character.

Who was Cooper? Was he all that he claimed to be? It's difficult to know for certain. However, at least some of what he stated can be corroborated by others. Other things, like his belief that Secret Service agent and limo driver William Greer shot JFK in Dallas, have been fully debunked. Individuals like the aforementioned Daniel Estulin and Dr. John Coleman, along with Dr. Dennis Cuddy and a number of others, are far more credible than Cooper. The following quotes from Cooper confirm what is already widely known..

> *The Knights of Malta is a world organization with its threads weaving through business, banking, politics, and CIA, other intelligence organizations, P2, religion, education, law, military, think tanks, foundations, the United States Information Agency, the United Nations, and numerous other organizations. They are not the oldest but one of the oldest branches of the Order of the Quest in existence. The world head of the Knights of Malta is elected for a life term, with the approval of the Pope. The Knights of Malta have their own Constitution and are sworn to work toward the establishment of a New World Order with the Pope at its head. Knights of Malta members are also powerful members of CFR and the Trilateral Commission.*[5]

But the individuals who have been (or are) part of the federal government are there for one purpose only. It is to overturn the current rule of law (as dictated by the Constitution) so that America can become a socialist state. One might ask, but what about the oath of office they took? Are they all liars? In a word, yes.

> *It is important that you know that the members of the Order take an oath that absolves them from any allegiance to any nation or king or government or constitution, and that includes the negating of any subsequent oath of allegiance which they may be required to take. They swear allegiance only to the Order and its goal of a New World Order. George Bush is not a loyal citizen of the United States but instead is loyal only to the*

---

[5] William Cooper, *Behold a Pale Horse* (1991), p. 86

> *destruction of the United States and to the formation of the New World Order. According to the oath Bush took when he was initiated into Skull & Bones, his oath of office as President of the United States of America means nothing.*[6]

This is obvious from the previous quote from Rockefeller alone. Every secret society has the same goal, which is ruling the world.

> *Many of them, however, disagree on exactly who will rule this New World Order, and that is what causes them to sometimes pull in opposite directions while nevertheless proceeding toward the same goal. The Vatican, for instance, wants the Pope to head the world coalition. Some want Lord Maitreya to head the New World Order. Lord Maitreya is the front runner, I believe, since witnesses say he was present on the ship at Malta with Bush, Gorbachev, and the ten regional heads of the New World Order.*[7]

The ten reigional heads of the NWO. Does this make you think of anything from either Daniel or Revelation? It should. The statue that Nebuchadnezzar saw in Daniel 2 had ten toes, which translated to ten horns in Revelation 17. In fact, the beast in Revelation 17 (with seven heads and ten horns) is the same beast that is referenced in Daniel 2 and 7. We will spend some time on that in upcoming chapters.

The incident in which Maitreya allegedly appeared and met with Bush and Gorbachev occurred during what is known as the Malta Summit in December 1989. Did it actually happen? I have no idea because there are no photographs or videos of the event. But Benjamin Crème's organization Share International highlights many aspects of Maitreya and firmly believes he is the next (and last) prophet to arrive to earth who will bring about world peace. They

---

[6] William Cooper, *Behold a Pale Horse* (1991), p. 82
[7] Ibid, p. 68

attest to the fact that Maitreya has appeared at various times and places throughout the world over the past few decades.

According to Cooper, whoever turns out to be the head of this coming world coalition would need to be approved by the Pope. This gives rise to the potentiality of the Pope being the second beast mentioned in Revelation 13:11ff. There, we learn that a second beast comes up out of the earth and has two small horns like a lamb, but speaks like a dragon. He has great authority equal to the first beast and causes the world to worship the first beast. It certainly could be somehow related to the Roman Catholic Church, but we have no way of knowing for sure until it actually happens and that second beast steps forward. Until then, it's all speculation.

In this section of Revelation, we also note that the second beast (whoever he may be – the Pope or someone else) gives his approval to the first beast and essentially works to cast the spotlight on the first beast. He brings life to the image of the beast and forces people to worship that image. Obviously, this second beast is important to the first beast, and taken together, this second beast plays the role of the counterfeit Holy Spirit who points to Jesus, who points to the Father. This true Trinity is counterfeited by Satan (who plays God the Father), the first beast/Antichrist (who portrays God the Son), and the second beast (who portrays God the Holy Spirit).

In creating his own image and counterfeit Trinity, Satan is doing all he can to prove that he is equal to God. He pulls out all the stops in doing so to fool as many people as possible and gather as many resources (natural and human) as possible to his side in the grand attempt to keep Jesus from physically returning to this earth in the future.

If you have heard anything about specific secret global societies, the one you may have heard about is the Bilderberg Group. They first formed in 1952 as a group, but remember, the people who formed this group had/have roots in numerous other secret socities. In that sense, the Bilderberg Group is only new by name, not by motives or intentions. According to many, this is the most powerful secret group in the world, ultimately created by Prince Bernhard of the Netherlands.

The original conference was held at the Hotel de Bilderberg in Oosterbeek, Netherlands, from 29 to 31 May 1954. It was initiated by several people, including Polish politician-in-exile Józef Retinger, concerned about the growth of anti-Americanism in Western Europe, who proposed an international conference at which leaders from European countries and the United States would be brought together with the aim of promoting Atlanticism – better understanding between the cultures of the United States and Western Europe to foster cooperation on political, economic and defense issues.

Retinger approached Prince Bernhard of the Netherlands who agreed to promote the idea, together with former Belgian Prime Minister Paul Van Zeeland, and the head of Unilever at that time, Dutchman Paul Rijkens. Bernhard in turn contacted Walter Bedell Smith, then head of the CIA, who asked Eisenhower adviser Charles Douglas Jackson to deal with the suggestion. The guest list was to be drawn up by inviting two attendees from each nation, one of each to represent conservative and liberal points of view. Fifty delegates from 11

> *countries in Western Europe attended the first conference, along with 11 Americans.*[8]

It does not matter what you or I personally believe about all of this. We may think that these secret societies are made up of crazy people simply spinning their wheels and accomplishing nothing. You may not believe in Satan, God, or ascended masters at all. The bottom line is that it really doesn't matter because those who participate in these secret societies at the top of the pyramid *do* believe in Satan as Lucifer and spend their lives in total dedication to him, attempting to gain the knowledge (and power that stems from it) that it is believed he possesses and wants to share with humanity.

What we will hopefully see as we continue through this book is how Satan (not these secret societies) is working diligently (and has been) to overcome every obstacle in his way so that he might set himself up as the physical ruler of this planet through his spiritual son, the coming Antichrist. That is the true goal of whatever Satan has attempted to accomplish in this world.

Unfortunately for those in these secret societies, they are, sadly, blinded to Satan's true purposes. They fully believe that they are following their own path that will place *them* in positions to rule over the earth.

Do you recall the mention of the ten regional heads of the NWO a few pages back? This is literally what the Global Elite are preparing for, and *if* Cooper's information is correct (we cannot know for certain), these ten regional heads have already been decided. These are the same kings mentioned in Revelation 17:12, which says:

> *The ten horns which you saw are ten kings who have not yet received a kingdom, but they receive authority as kings with the beast for one hour.*

---

[8] http://en.wikipedia.org/wiki/Bilderberg_Group (4/15/2014)

Here they were in 1989, on a ship with Bush, Gorbachev, and allegedly Maitreya, the one whom many will receive as The Christ, returned to earth to reign. The ten regional heads of the coming NWO were also part of that summit. Do you find that fascinating?

The Bible says they will not rule until they receive a kingdom and authority to rule as kings for *one hour*. Their time to rule will be granted to them ultimately by God Himself.

The reference to "one hour" may be due to the fact that their reign ends up being so short in duration. Daniel 7:8 states, *"While I was contemplating the horns, behold, another horn, a little one, came up among them, and three of the first horns were pulled out by the roots before it; and behold, this horn possessed eyes like the eyes of a man and a mouth uttering great boasts."*

The use of "one hour" reminds us of when Jesus said His hour had not yet come to his mother at the wedding at Cana (cf. John 2). Certainly, He was not saying that his "hour" would only be an hour. He was saying that the specific time when His ministry was to begin had not yet arrived.

Daniel sees the ten horns, then another little horn (an eleventh) comes up out of the ten. Apparently, this eleventh horn kills three of the original ten horns (and becomes the eighth), leaving seven. Certainly, the fact that three of the ten horns have just been killed by the little horn signals to the remaining seven that they'd better go along with the Antichrist or be killed themselves!

Their short ("one hour") reign is over at that point. They are allowed to live in exchange for their loyalty. Antichrist becomes supreme ruler and the remaining seven kings become his inner circle of servants.

We've shared a great deal in this chapter and some of it might be confusing. Don't worry, as we will go into more detail in upcoming chapters, and we will start with what we can learn from Daniel 2.

While these secret societies believe leaders among them will rule, that is merely the lie that Satan has beguiled them with because in the end, Satan will rule through the Antichrist, his spiritual son. That's what it's all about. It's not the Global Elite ruling. They're simply pawns being used to set up the system that Satan needs in order to prove that he is able to be "like the Most High."

The Global Elite, through the plethora of secret societies, has one goal. That goal is to rule the world. They cannot see anything beyond that because Satan has blinded them to his true goals and aspirations. He and he alone will rule, but in order to do so, he needs minions loyal to him to do his work to set up the one-world system that he will ultimately use. They're his slaves but don't know it.

Again though, even though he will rule (for seven years; the duration of the coming Tribulation), that is simply the means to the end. Once he gains control of the entire world, with all resources and people, he will be able to do whatever it takes to become "like the Most High."

Unfortunately, both for Satan and the people who have fallen for his lies, he will fail miserably in the end. He is no match for God the Son, Jesus, and when He returns to this earth, the first thing He will do is destroy the man of lawlessness (2 Thessalonians 2) with the breath of His mouth.

Chapter 4
Daniel 2: Before Rome Began

One of the things that I find absolutely fascinating is the fact that a good deal of the Bible was written as *prophecy*. That makes sense because when books of the Bible were originally written, many of the things they speak of had not yet occurred.

God chose to provide people with knowledge of His plan that included world events often long before they happened. To me, this is one of the greatest proofs of God's existence as well as His sovereignty.

Though so-called "higher critics" have done their level best to pan, criticize, and even castigate the Bible as being completely unreliable, the truth of history bears out the fact that what God has said *will* happen, *has* happened. The things that have not yet occurred simply await His timing, but we can be assured – due to God's perfect track record – that all things will come about just as He has said they will.

Even the critics, when dealing with a book like Daniel, can only say that because it is so accurate, it must have been written by someone only claiming to be "Daniel" but who actually wrote *after* many of the events occurred in that book. This is disingenuous because many of the events had not (and still have not) occurred yet in history. They remain in front of us as yet-to-be-fulfilled events.

As for Rome, long before Romulus and Remus even lived on this planet, an ancient ruler (Nebuchadnezzar) saw the Roman Empire laid out before him in a dream given to Him by God. In the book of Daniel, chapter two, we read about the dream that King Nebuchadnezzar dreamt one night. It unnerved this very powerful and fearless king and he naturally wanted to know what it meant.

Nebuchadnezzar called all of his wise men and insisted that they tell him what he had dreamed. Only after they had told him what the dream was would he allow them to interpret it (if they were correct). Of course, the wise men were perplexed at such a request and insisted that no one could do what the king was asking.

But Nebuchadnezzar would not be put off. If they couldn't tell him what he had dreamed along with the interpretation, they would all be executed. It was at this point that Daniel was brought in to the king. Daniel said that the God he worshipped could certainly do what Nebuchadnezzar was asking and if Daniel and his friends could be given some time to ask God for the information the king sought, they would be able to tell him.

Nebuchadnezzar temporarily relented and allowed them some time. Daniel and his friends (Shadrach, Meshach, and Abed-Nego) prayed and God responded. Daniel went in to the king and told him what he had dreamed and what it all meant (Daniel 2:31-35):

> *You, O king, were looking and behold, there was a single great statue; that statue, which was large and of extraordinary splendor, was standing in front of you, and its appearance was awesome. The head of that statue was made of fine gold, its breast and its arms of silver, its belly and its thighs of bronze, its legs of iron, its feet partly of iron and partly of clay. You continued looking until a stone was cut out without hands, and it struck the statue on its feet of iron and clay and crushed them. Then the iron, the clay, the bronze, the silver and the gold were crushed all at the same time and became like chaff from the summer threshing floors; and the wind carried them away so that not a trace of them was found. But the stone that struck the statue became a great mountain and filled the whole earth.*

Notice Daniel points out that the king was "looking" and saw the statue. God provided Nebuchadnezzar a dream and he saw various empires laid out before him from Babylon to the end of time. He saw them from the human perspective and that is important to understand because in other chapters of Daniel, we will see the same scenario, but from God's perspective.

Nebuchadnezzar was impressed with Daniel's ability and rewarded him by putting him in charge of all the wise men. Of course, this caused some jealously, but that's another story. For now, we know that Nebuchadnezzar knew the information he received from Daniel was true because the king knew what he dreamed and would be able to know if Daniel was lying to him by making something up or if Daniel's God was powerful enough to reveal the dream and the interpretation to Daniel.

But what were the meanings of all the details of the dream? Daniel explains the meaning of the dream in Daniel 2:36-38. Essentially, Nebuchadnezzar dreamed of a large statue that had a head of gold, arms and chest of silver, belly and thighs of bronze, and legs of iron.

> *This was the dream; now we will tell its interpretation before the king. You, O king, are the king of kings, to whom the God of heaven has given the kingdom, the power, the strength and the glory; and wherever the sons of men dwell, or the beasts of the field, or the birds of the sky, He has given them into your hand and has caused you to rule over them all. You are the head of gold.*

But that's not the end of the statue or the dream. The rest of it is explained by Daniel as well. These kingdoms turn out to be Babylon, the Medo-Persian, the Grecian, and the Roman empires, in that order (Daniel 2:39-43).

> *After you there will arise another kingdom inferior to you, then another third kingdom of bronze, which will rule over all the earth. Then there will be a fourth kingdom as strong as iron; inasmuch as iron crushes and shatters all things, so, like iron that breaks in pieces, it will crush and break all these in pieces. In that you saw the feet and toes, partly of potter's clay and partly of iron, it will be a divided kingdom; but it will have in it the toughness of iron, inasmuch as you saw the iron mixed with common clay. As the toes of the feet were partly of iron and partly of pottery, so some of the kingdom will be strong and part of it will be brittle. And in that you saw the iron mixed with common clay, they will combine with one another in the seed of men; but they will not adhere to one another, even as iron does not combine with pottery.*

As noted in the text, the feet including the toes are mixed with clay and iron. We learn through the remainder of chapter two of Daniel that each section of the statue represents a different kingdom. To recap, we see the following empires represented by various metals:

- *Head of gold – Babylonian Empire*
- *Arms and chest of silver – Medo-Persian Empire*
- *Belly and thighs of bronze – Grecian Empire*
- *Legs of Iron – Roman Empire*
- *Rock that crushes – Messianic Kingdom*

What is interesting here is that while the legs represent the Roman Empire, the feet and toes represent the *coming Revised* Roman Empire (or final stage of it). In order to understand this, we need to look at some maps and a brief history of each kingdom and learn how one kingdom segued into the next. We will do this in an upcoming chapter.

Here's something else to consider, and it may be difficult for you to believe. I suggest doing your own research. Authors John Klein and Adam Spears discuss the iron mixing with clay as referenced by the toes of the statue.

> *According to Hebraic symbology, clay is the sign for man. Indeed, the word 'Adamah' (whence comes the name 'Adam'; this, within the first man's name is a direct reference to where he came from) literally means 'soil,' and iron is the sign for angels operating on the earth. Therefore, within the Kingdom of the Beast, Daniel is prophesying that there will once again be a comingling between man and devils.*
>
> *In other words, just as Yeshua said in Luke 17:26-27, this familiar passage from Daniel, written long before Yeshua came the*

> *first time, is prophesying that teraphim[9] will be having intercourse and producing offspring as they did in the days of Noah, just before Yeshua comes back for the final time.*[10]

The point is that these two authors believe that, according to statements by Jesus, we will see a bit of a replay of what occurred in Genesis 6 when fallen angels (specifically, teraphim) mated somehow with human women. The result was the Nephilim.

This also ties nicely in with Satan's goals of world dominance. As his power builds throughout the various kingdoms and incarnations of the final Roman Empire, he is gathering as much power to himself as he can. To have Nephilim standing with him at the same time is only a plus for him.

The various kingdoms, beginning with Babylon, start the clock ticking for a period of time the Bible refers to as the Times of the Gentiles (Luke 21; Romans 11; see also Ezekiel 30; Isaiah 17, 62; Revelation 11). While the Egyptian and Assyrian empires existed *prior* to the Babylonian Empire, it was with the kingdom of Babylon that God started the clock ticking with respect to Israel and Jerusalem and the Times of the Gentiles.

It was from the time of Nebuchadnezzar's conquering of Jerusalem and forward when God decreed that Jerusalem would be controlled by Gentile nations and that they would tread Jerusalem under foot until the Times of the Gentiles had ended. I believe we are still living in that time period. Further, I believe this time period will end when Jesus physically returns.

---

[9] Teraphim are the lowest order of angels and can take on human form for extended periods of time (according to Klein and Spears)

[10] John Klein/Adam Spears *Lost in Translation, Volume 1* (2007), p. 104

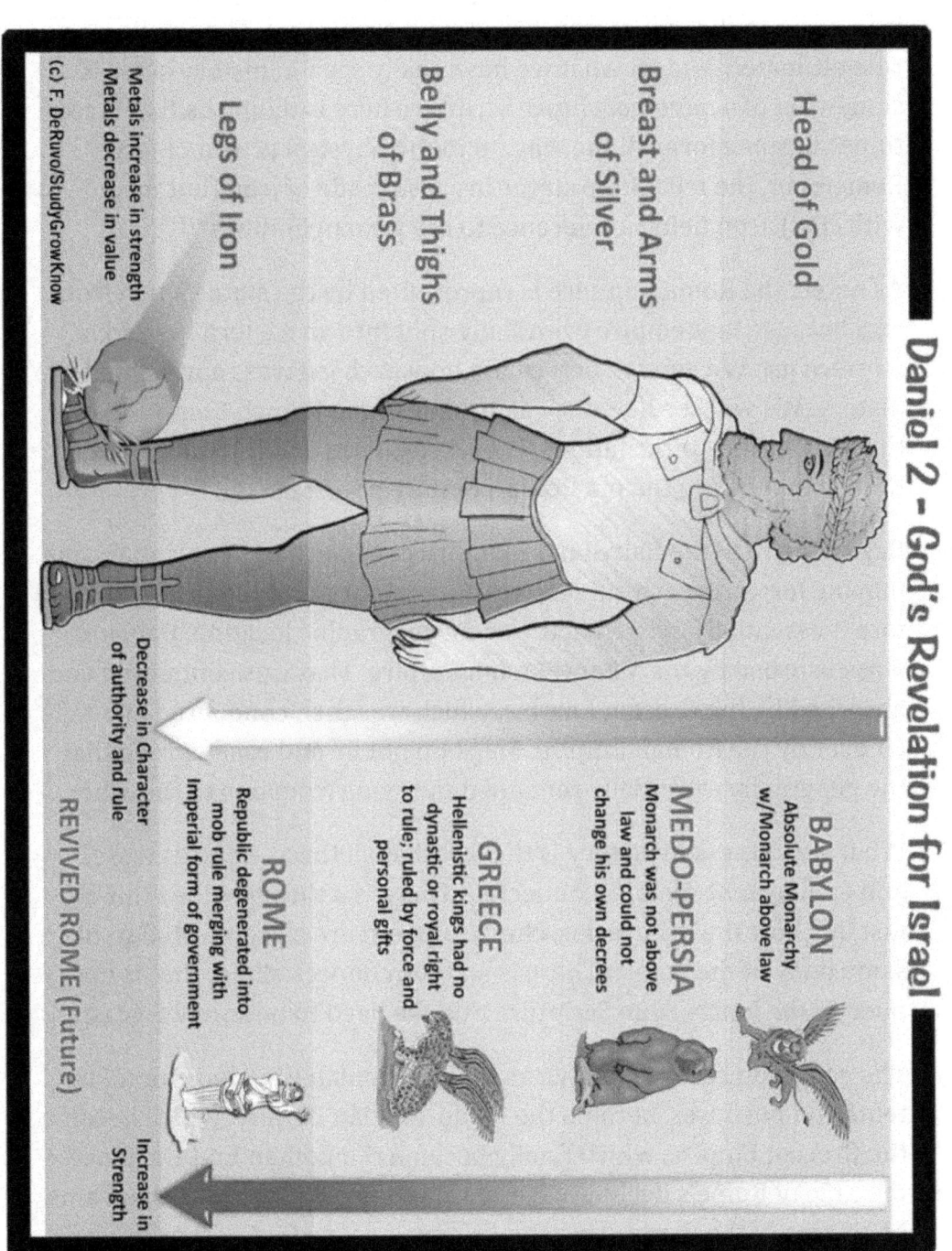

The final empire is the Roman Empire, represented by the legs of iron down to the feet of iron mixed with clay (toes). Though Roman rule ultimately ended, what we have really seen in history since is somewhat of a *metamorphosis*. Scripture here is telling us that it continues in some form all the way up to the physical return of Jesus. Remember, the feet of the statue are also made of iron (but mixed with clay), iron being a reference to the Roman Empire.

As noted, the Roman Empire is represented by the statue's two iron legs because that empire eventually split into an eastern leg and a western leg. We need to determine how each leg was represented in history. We will see how the eastern leg of the Roman Empire went through various incarnations. We will also see that the same type of thing happened to the old Roman Empire's western leg.

Beginning with the Babylonian Empire of Nebuchadnezzar's day and moving forward, each successive empire that uprooted the one before it essentially existed in the same geographic location. Babylon was absorbed by the Medo-Persian Empire. That was conquered and absorbed by the Grecian Empire, which was then conquered and taken over by the Roman Empire. Maps do not lie and easily prove that the geography essentially remained the same from one to the other.

What we witness in history is the fact that all these empires were, and to an extent remain, connected. There is a through line. This is just like how the head, arms, chest, legs, etc. are all connected to the same body of the statue. There is an interconnectedness that is implied in the image from Scripture that we need to be sure we grasp.

The geographical area known as the Babylonian Kingdom, for all intents and purposes, became the Medo-Persian Empire, which became the Grecian Empire, which finally became the Roman Empire. Since the time of Rome's decline, several things have occurred in that same basic area of the world. This shows how it segued into other things but the geography remained the same. We need to spend some time looking at what happened and how things ended up.

As the Roman Empire diminished in strength until it had ultimately become a mere shadow of what it had been at the peak of its power, other entities, like the Ottoman Empire, which was Islamic in nature, took over. From there, other changes occurred through to today.

Though the Ottoman Empire declined, it was eventually replaced with parts of the European Union (EU). However, in this case, Islam did not cease to exist and that is extremely important to understand. Islam came into being via Muhammad and eventually turned into a (known) world caliphate[11] via the Ottoman Empire, which stretched all the way to Spain (as did the Roman Empire). Though the Ottoman Empire is gone, many of the countries that were part of that empire continue to exist and maintain an Islamic emphasis.

Today, though the Ottoman Empire is long gone, with the EU remaining as the main "empire" in Europe, Islam continues to exist and pursue its goal of becoming another caliphate. Muslims believe that this next (and last) caliphate will rule through the appearance of what they call Final Mahdi (aka Antichrist in Christianity).

In essence then, Islam, though not having its own empire currently, is simply taking over bits and pieces of the world as more people become Muslims, or as Sharia law goes into effect. Eventually, there will be enough Muslims with enough power to simply create their own caliphate. We will explore this more later, but I firmly believe that this is the reason so much of the world (and especially the world's leaders) seem to turn a blind eye to the problems that Islam creates. While average citizens rebel at the partiality shown to Islam, political leaders *seem* oblivious. I don't believe this to be accidental.

---

[11] an Islamic state led by a supreme religious and political leader known as a caliph

We have presented a very brief, truncated history of Rome's development from one village to a full-blown Empire. Obviously, not all details about Rome's advancement could be included and that's not what this book is designed to do. However, if we were to present a thoroughly detailed history of how the Roman Empire developed over several hundred years, we would see a slow growth coupled with failures and defeats, with more growth through victories, then more defeats.

This would be the case until Rome finally found its footing in history and began to defeat one area of the known world after another, absorbing each new area into the Roman Empire. This is how Rome grew into the biblical beast it became.

Using the Grecian Empire as an example, we can truly say that rarely do empires grow as quickly as Alexander's did. Most of the time, it takes numerous false starts before an empire even begins to take shape. It is often the same when that empire falls and another begins to take its place. The false starts, followed by some victories here and there, with more defeats in between, appear to be the norm more often than not.

With respect to Rome and the resultant Roman Empire, though historians often cite a fairly definitive end date for Rome, in reality, the Roman Empire took quite some time to be fully extinguished. Even then, one can easily argue that based on past history and what other empires went through (seguing from one to the next), it is quite logical to say that the Roman Empire went through a metamorphosis which will continue until it reaches its final state.

This final state is really the Revised Roman Empire at some point in the future from where we sit today. Timothy C. Hall notes that *"476 is traditionally considered the date of the fall of the Roman Empire, but* *the **eastern** portion of the Roman Empire, under the capital city of Constantinople, continued for 1,000 years as the Byzantine Empire."*[12]

At least part of the Roman Empire continued until approximately AD 1453. While the Germanic tribes chipped away and caused the western leg of the Roman Empire to fall, they undoubtedly absorbed aspects of that part of the Roman Empire into what became their empire.

Just as importantly, what we need to consider are the *traits* of the Roman Empire, compared to the traits of the final version of this fourth beast. The same principles that guided the Roman Empire will exist to guide the final version represented by the toes mixed with iron and clay. As Rome had one ultimate ruler, so will the final phase of this fourth beast also have one ultimate ruler. That is the characteristic that we need to see.

But where – if anywhere – do we get the idea from Scripture that though this fourth beast (Rome) died out, it eventually rises again? Is there something there that tells us that Rome will essentially rise again in the last days prior to the return of Jesus Christ? Can we specify this metamorphosis into the final form from the Biblical record?

I fully believe there are numerous places in Scripture where God enlightens us to the plans of the enemy and where He conclusively shows that the old Roman Empire will rise again, in the same geographical area where it existed originally. From there, it will grow to cover the entire world and will have one Imperial ruler over the entire empire (the world). That ruler will be the Antichrist.

We will deal with these passages of Scripture in upcoming chapters.

---

[12] Timothy C. Hall, *The Complete Idiot's Guide to World History* (2012), p. 72 (emphasis added)

Chapter 5

Do Empires Really Die?

Many may not be aware of the fact that part of Ancient Rome included a vibrant wine center in Italy near Pompeii. It is clear from archaeological evidence that the area below Mount Vesuvius (including Pompeii) was rich in natural resources and fertile for producing crops for the people of the Roman Empire. *"Wine, in particular, was a valuable export for this prosperous region, supporting trade connections as far as Britannia and India."*[13]

If you know your history, you also know that in AD 79, Mount Vesuvius erupted, raining molten death and ash onto the areas below the

---

[13] http://popular-archaeology.com/issue/03012014/article/digging-on-the-dark-side-of-vesuvius (3/21/2014)

mount. Thousands were killed, encased in ash-laden coffins that captured the final moments of their lives as they attempted to flee the destruction. The entire geographical region below Mount Vesuvius was destroyed, and the vineyards with it.

This destruction occurred only nine years after the Roman armies surrounded and ultimately destroyed Jerusalem along with the Jewish Temple. Was this God's judgment? If it wasn't, it certainly did not help the Roman Empire.

Pompeii was a city where Rome's elite enjoyed going to vacation and play. Hedonism was most certainly part of the Roman Empire, especially among the elite. For the wealthy, getting away from the headquarters of the empire even for a few days at a time was just what they needed. There was plenty to do in Pompeii.

The Latin word *lupa* was used to reference a prostitute in Rome and a brothel was a *lupanar*. The most well-known brothel of Pompeii was called the *Lupanar of Pompeii*. Archaeologists believe that ancient Pompeii had up to 35 brothels. These, of course, were for the ordinary citizens and residents. The wealthy had their own mistresses or slaves so they would not need to frequent brothels or bathhouses.

What is fascinating is to see just how often not only empires but individual cities and villages throughout history would experience God's wrath due to their own level of debauchery that too often went unchecked. Such was certainly the case with Sodom and Gomorrah (Genesis 19). It was also the case with cities like Nineveh even though the town initially repented due to the preaching of Jonah. Eventually, they fell back into their old ways of caving to the sins of lust and pleasure and were destroyed 50 years later.

It was also the same with Jerusalem when they continued on a wayward path that rejected God. His patience ended when the leaders of

Israel rejected God the Son, Jesus. Jesus Himself prophesied Jerusalem's destruction in His Olivet Discourse of Matthew 24. This is a recurring theme through the Hebrew Bible (Old Testament) as well as various places throughout the New Testament books like Revelation.

But it wasn't necessarily the debauchery of a group of people in a town or area that forced God to rain down His wrath upon them. Sometimes it had to do with the way they treated His people of Israel, whom He personally described as the "apple of His eye."

We look to Zechariah 2:8-9a, which states very clearly: *"For this is what the Lord Almighty says: 'After the Glorious One has sent me against the nations that have plundered you—for whoever touches you touches the apple of his eye— I will surely raise my hand against them so that their slaves will plunder them'."*

This particular passage is looking ahead to an event from Zechariah's point of view and even toward the very end of human history prior to the physical return of Jesus. At the same time, we also know that the principle that God outlines in that passage is something He puts into effect whenever He deems it necessary where Israel is concerned.

When Israel rejected their Messiah – Jesus – God used the Roman Empire to mete out His judgment against Israel, that nation of rebels. Judgment came in AD 70. It is logical to conclude that just as He had done in the past with other nations, God began to pour out His wrath on the Roman Empire for how they treated Israel, even though they were used by God as His arm of reprimand against Israel.

That may sound a bit confusing or even unfair, but the truth of the matter is that God's ways are not man's ways. As God and Creator, His actions perfectly suit His purposes and bring Him glory. This is somewhat difficult for us to see because we are often blinded by the sin nature that resides within us.

The eruption of Italy's Mount Vesuvius may well have been one instance of God's wrath in a line of many forthcoming instances. Over time, Rome would fall, as it went the way of every other kingdom and empire before it.

However, the Bible tells us that a particular "beast" (represented as either a leader, kingdom, or both) fully appears to be dead, but then comes back to life. This is explained in Revelation 13. Is this referring to a kingdom or an individual? I believe it's referring to a kingdom primarily, but obviously an individual is fully identified with that kingdom (the Antichrist).

But if this "kingdom" died and comes back to life, which kingdom is it referring to here? Could it be the Roman Empire?

Consider the fact that from the time of the Babylonian Kingdom through to and including the Roman Empire, one empire after another replaced the previous one in virtually the same geographical location. In essence, a new empire took over the old one and with it new cultures, new languages, and new customs *blended* with the previous ones. We get a sense of this in Revelation 13:2-3.

> *And the beast which I saw was like a leopard, and his feet were like those of a bear, and his mouth like the mouth of a lion. And the dragon gave him his power and his throne and great authority. I saw one of his heads as if it had been slain, and his fatal wound was healed. And the whole earth was amazed and followed after the beast.*

Notice in the above text that this particular beast (empire) has aspects of the previous beasts or empires. Elements of previous empires segued into the new empire simply because people from that previous empire remained. While leaders and rulers can be replaced with new leaders and rulers, all the vestiges of the previous administration are not eradicated. That's true of anything.

Overall, this particular beast was like a leopard but also had feet like a bear and a mouth like a lion. Bear's feet are powerful, firmly planted on the earth, allowing it to rear up on its hind legs. A swipe from a bear's paw can do tremendous damage, even killing. Each beast represents the different empires.

A lion (Babylon) has an unmistakable roar that all animals recognize. When it is heard, animals will run for fear of being killed and eaten. The lion is the king of the forest and all animals know it. They recognize the power of the lion and the bear.

The leopard (Greece), of course, signals speed, and apparently this final empire that comes after the old Roman Empire grows at a very fast pace. The inherent power and ability to deceive (through lies and coercion) is like a magnet to people. The fact that it (the beast, representing a kingdom) appears to have been slain (one of his heads or empires, as if it had been slain) makes this beast even more attractive to people.

I realize that many people believe that this "head" refers to a person, the Antichrist. In reality, John is talking about a "head" that represents a particular beast or empire. Certainly there is a leader for each empire that has occurred in history and without that particular individual the empire would likely not have existed. At the same time, the Bible here appears to be describing the nature of the empire itself.

The Roman Empire was not led by one individual throughout its reign. Many Caesars came and went. Many other rulers and leaders took part in ruling over parts of the Roman Empire. We should note that the Roman Empire was really the first empire to have something like this.

The Babylonian Empire was ruled by one man, Nebuchadnezzar (Imperialism). The Medo-Persian Empire was ruled by two rulers, at different times (Imperialism). The Grecian Empire was ruled initially by

Alexander and after his death the empire was divided into four parts, ruled by generals, but still remained the Grecian Empire.

The Roman Empire instituted something completely new with more of a democracy, ruled by various leaders over time. The length of the Roman Empire's reign meant that it wasn't tied to one particular person, but to an ideology, a way of thinking. This is what made the Roman Empire different from all the others. As one Caesar died, he was simply replaced with another.

At the same time, the final version of the fourth empire (or beast) that emerges from all the previous empires is unique and different from the others. Daniel 7:1-7 gives us a more detailed look at the beasts, including the final version of the fourth beast. Pay careful attention to the comparisons. I believe these descriptions are from God's perspective.

> *In the first year of Belshazzar king of Babylon Daniel saw a dream and visions in his mind as he lay on his bed; then he wrote the dream down and related the following summary of it. Daniel said, "I was looking in my vision by night, and behold, the four winds of heaven were stirring up the great sea. And four great beasts were coming up from the sea, different from one another. The first was like a lion and had the wings of an eagle. I kept looking until its wings were plucked, and it was lifted up from the ground and made to stand on two feet like a man; a human mind also was given to it. And behold, another beast, a second one, resembling a bear. And it was raised up on one side, and three ribs were in its mouth between its teeth; and thus they said to it, 'Arise, devour much meat!' After this I kept looking, and behold, another one, like a leopard, which had on its back four wings of a bird; the beast also had four heads, and dominion was given to it. After this I kept looking in the night visions,*

> *and behold, a fourth beast, dreadful and terrifying and extremely strong; and it had large iron teeth. It devoured and crushed and trampled down the remainder with its feet; and it was different from all the beasts that were before it, and it had ten horns.*

Notice that each empire was different from the one before it. So it was with each new successive empire. Nebuchadnezzar's Babylonian Kingdom segued into the Medo-Persian Empire, and then came Alexander the Great, who conquered and took over the Medes and Persians.

There is no way to entirely sweep away all that remains from the previous empire, and who would want to do that? Each new empire was different because it had its own character, customs, and even language, but still incorporated aspects of the previous empire as well. It really could not be all wiped away.

As each new ruler rose up to take his place in history, he would decide which aspects of the previous empire he would keep and which he would toss out. This is why the Bible indicates that each new empire absorbed aspects of the previous empire and each previous empire "lived" on in the newly installed empire.

By the time the Roman Empire took its position in history, features of each of the previous empires remained. But Roman rule added new things to the empire upon which it had built itself, making it different than all previous empires.

Notice the text we've just quoted that references the Roman Empire. "*After this I kept looking in the night visions, and behold, a fourth beast, dreadful and terrifying and extremely strong; and it had large* **iron teeth**. *It devoured and crushed and trampled down the remainder with its feet; and it was different from all the beasts that were before it, and it had ten horns*" (emphasis added).

This empire is *"dreadful and terrifying and extremely strong."* Iron teeth? The legs of Nebuchadnezzar's statue were made of iron. It had such ferocity that it crushed and trampled down the remainder of previous empires with its feet. Notice also that this empire was different from all previous beasts because it had ten horns. This appears to be the final stage of the fourth beast, and that has not yet happened in history.

I believe what is being explained here are the changes the Roman Empire – the fourth beast – goes through as it segues into the "feet" of the statue in Daniel 2. This will occur at the end of this age. (Taking a cue from the Jewish sages, there are two ages: the age we are living in now and the next age – the Messianic Age – when Messiah reigns.)

The Roman Empire was different from previous beasts because of the way it ran its government. It was strong and trampled anything in its path, having its own ferocious character and nature. The final stage of the fourth beast is really the Roman Empire come back to life. But how is this going to occur?

The revitalized Roman Empire will ultimately be led by one man (after the ten kings are given opportunity to rule), just as previous empires were. Ultimately, one man at a time led the Roman Empire, and empires previous to Rome were also led by one man.

Then why is there reference to ten horns? These ten horns represent ten leaders who will initially control the final stage of the fourth beast (in its revitalized form). However, from those ten leaders (kings), the Antichrist will rise and will "subdue" (kill) three of them. As the *eleventh* (one rising up out of the ten, but not part of the ten), he kills three and then becomes the imperial ruler (he is then the *eighth* out of the seven remaining, Revelation 17:11).

Thus, the Roman Empire, though it appears to have died in history, will be resurrected (happening now) and will have one ruler over all.

This "all" will include the entire world, not simply Europe or Asia or some "known world." The Antichrist will rule the entire world and this has never been accomplished before at any point in history.

While individual men and women have ruled the "known world" or parts of it, only the Antichrist will be given absolute power to control the entire world. He will be the final ruler of the globe prior to the return of Jesus. Ironic to consider the fact that in 2014, we are moving toward a time when one person will rule the entire world!

We also notice, of course, that each of the previous empires before the Roman Empire, though having been conquered, really did not completely cease to exist (Revelation 13), and that is a very important point that we need to keep at the forefront as we go through our study. Nothing really died.

The newly conquered empire was absorbed into the new empire that replaced it. Even though the fourth beast, the Roman Empire, is said to destroy everything that came before it, it still absorbed a good deal. The power and might of Rome simply eradicated the memories of previous empires for that period of time.

Let's put this in terms of corporations and companies. How often have we read about some corporation taking over a smaller corporation or company? In the process, the larger corporation that has taken over the smaller one usually sends in new management people. The old management is gone and now employees are faced with the uncertainty of what the new managers will expect.

Most of the time, the new management will simply allow that newly acquired company to continue on as normal. Over time, these new managers will begin to inject new thought and possibly new direction into that newly purchased company. However, it is very rare for the new management to come in, wipe out the entire workforce and

Original plastic model kits produced by the most well-known model-making company from the 1960s (for figure kits). Though original kits are hard to find, they have been reissued by numerous model companies after Aurora assets were sold by Nabisco.

move the smaller company in a brand new direction. This usually only happens when that newly purchased company is failing.

More often than not, the company continues as it has been going and new management seeks to mainly make the newly acquired company more profitable for the corporation that just bought it.

For instance, one of my favorite companies of my youth was the old Aurora Plastics Corporation from the 1960s. They produced some of the best plastic figure models known to kid-dom. Frankenstein, Wolfman, Dracula, Batman, Spiderman, and a host of other 1:8 scale figure kits, complete with bases, were made available to kids my age and we spent hours building and painting these scenes that reminded us of the shows we watched on TV and the comics we read.

Aurora was eventually purchased by Nabisco, the food giant. As usual, they got rid of the existing management of Aurora and brought their own people in. They made the decisions as to how the company was to be run and in general allowed things to continue much as they had when Aurora owned the company.

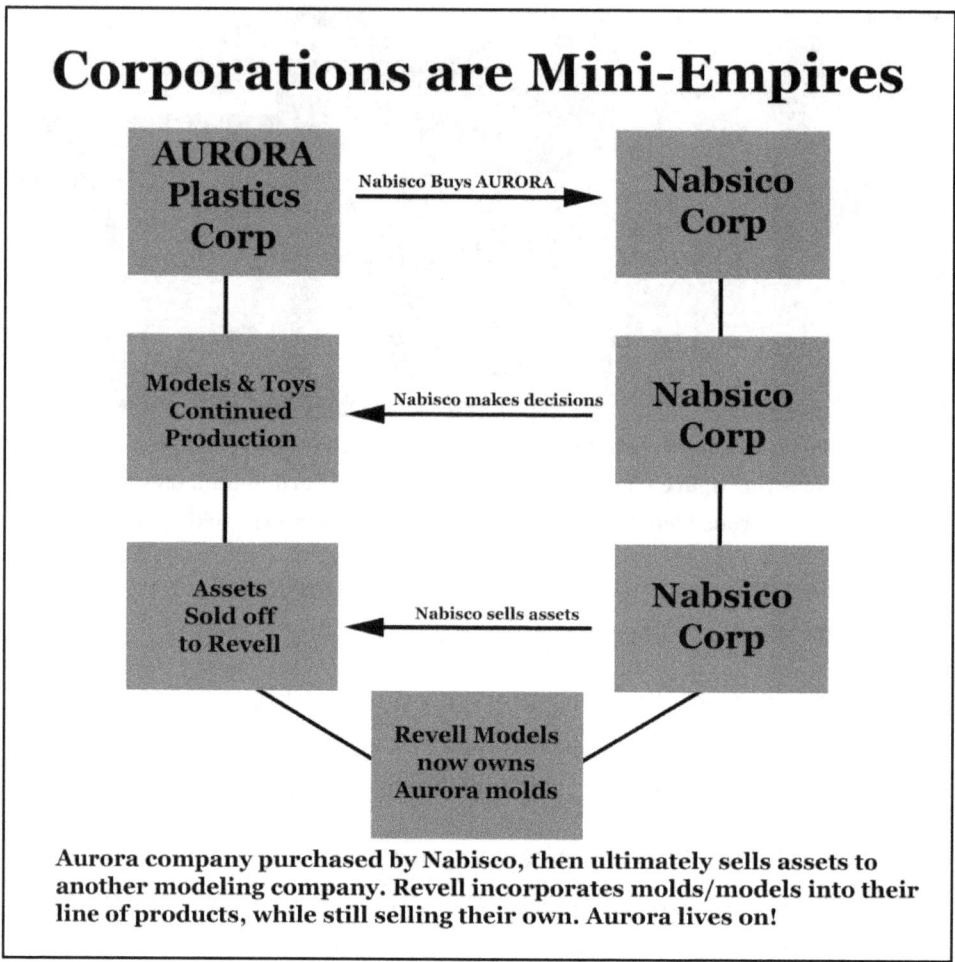

Aurora company purchased by Nabisco, then ultimately sells assets to another modeling company. Revell incorporates molds/models into their line of products, while still selling their own. Aurora lives on!

However, when the first controversy arose from some of the model kits the company was producing, these execs had to make a decision. They canceled that particular line of model kits. This was the 1970s and society was changing. Nabisco didn't want the negative publicity from protestors who thought Aurora's models were too violent or sexist.

Over time, Nabisco refined and even *redefined* Aurora so that models once sold by the crate previously were being shelved. More toys came out instead of models. Nabisco did things the *safe* way, but lost consumers in the process.

 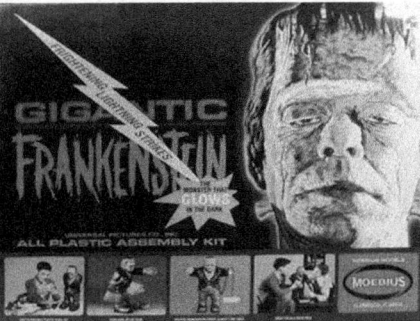 

Three Frankenstein plastic model kits. The Luminators was reissued by Monogram in translucent orange plastic (left). The Gigantic Frankenstein was reissued by Moebius Models and the Bonus Value Pack Frankenstein was reissued by Monogram and also came with paints and glue. Aurora lived on!

Eventually, the modeling fad began to die out because things like computer games from Atari were taking the place of models. Boys didn't want to sit around a workbench smelling glue and painting models anymore. Computer games were more fun.

But even though modeling seemed to die out, it really never did. The molds for these old models were eventually purchased by Revell-Monogram Modeling Company (when Aurora's assets were sold off by Nabisco). The molds were put in storage but eventually saw the light of day again when Revell-Monogram began to reissue them under their logo. Some were also later reissued by Moebius Models.

Those of us who modeled when we were boys took notice and bought the reissued kits, and once again the modeling hobby was alive and well. Because of it, more companies began producing original figure kits like the old Aurora Company had produced.

In fact, this opened up a whole new arena. Companies referred to as "garage kit" businesses (because the kits were made in someone's garage out of rubber molds with resin, instead of plastic) also began popping up. They reissued some of the old Aurora kits and also produced their own by hiring sculptors to create new kits.

Totally new Batman concepts issued by Revell (Val Kilmer as Batman), Moebius (Christian Bale), Revell (Jim Carrey as Riddler), Moebius (Julie Newmar as Catwoman and Adam West as Batman from the 1966 TV classic). If not for Aurora, these kits would likely never have been produced.

From this, magazines dedicated to the craft of building and painting figure models came into being, and from there, garage kit expos began popping up all over the country. Though Aurora Plastics Corporation had "died," figure kits continued.

The figure kit market also expanded greatly, then waned again after roughly 10 to 15 years. However, figure kits can still be purchased today from a number of smaller companies. The figure kits are produced in high-grade plastic and are along the lines of the quality of kits that Aurora Plastics Corporation used to produce.

Since Aurora issued figure model kits in the early 1960s, things have gone full circle, and now, roughly 50 years later, figure kits are still being produced by other companies that took their cue from Aurora. In essence, though the Aurora Plastics Company went through several changes on its own, it was eventually bought by another company and then its assets sold. However, as noted, Aurora continues to "live" through other companies today that are doing exactly what Aurora used to do.

It is the same principle when any company buys another company. It's also true when an empire is conquered by another empire in history. All the remnants of that conquered empire are not eradicated by the new empire. Bits and pieces are kept alive by the leaders and rulers of the new empire. They never start from scratch and many aspects of a conquered empire are kept intact and become part of the new empire. It's just the way things work in the world.

Chapter 6
All the Same Geography

In order to make our point from the previous chapter even more clear, let's take a few moments to look at the geographical areas of several empires leading up to the Roman Empire. If you're like me, seeing a visual is always more effective because it not only helps me remember something, but it does so because it makes a greater impact on my brain.

If we start with Babylon, the empire that Nebuchadnezzar built (with God's permission), we can clearly see the extent of that empire. Since a huge mountain range was in the way, requiring him to go up and around, Nebuchadnezzar conquered Jerusalem from the north, not the east. He made several trips back and forth to Jerusalem from Babylon during these raids against Jerusalem. Over the course of these incursions into Jerusalem, he also took many of the artifacts from the Jewish Temple that the Jewish people used in service and worship to God. These he stored in his treasury back in Babylon. It ultimately kept the Temple vessels safe, at least until Belshazzar.

But let's look at the area of the Babylonian Empire. This empire was represented by the head of gold from the statue in Daniel 2. It went from roughly 606 BC to 536 BC before being conquered and taken over by the Medes and Persians.

We also know from the Bible (Daniel 5) what the event was that precipitated God's judgment on the Babylonian Empire. Here, we read that Nebuchadnezzar's grandson, Belshazzar (king at this time), decided to have a party for 1,000 of his nobles. During the course of the party, Belshazzar apparently thought it would be a great idea to send for the *"gold and silver vessels which Nebuchadnezzar his father had taken out of the temple which was in Jerusalem, so that the king and his nobles, his wives and his concubines might drink from them"* (Daniel 5:2). Not as great an idea as Belshazzar originally thought, as we shall see.

As far as God was concerned, this was not a brilliant move because it would desecrate these items. Not long after Belshazzar and his guests began drinking from the vessels (that had been safely stored in the treasury up until that time), a disembodied hand began writing on the wall the words, "MENĒ, MENĒ, TEKĒL, UPHARSIN." It took Daniel to gain the knowledge of the interpretation of the words and, more specifically, how those words applied to Belshazzar.

Of course, Belshazzar could read the words and he understood their meaning because they were in his language. What he failed to understand is how the words *applied* to him. What did they mean for him as king? Daniel explained that meaning to him.

> *God has numbered your kingdom and put an end to it. 'TEKĒL'—you have been weighed on the scales and found deficient. 'PERĒS'—your kingdom has been divided and given over to the Medes and Persians.* (Daniel 5:26-28)

Verses 30 and 31 of Daniel 5 explain what happened next. "*That same night Belshazzar the Chaldean king was slain. So Darius the Mede received the kingdom at about the age of sixty-two.*"

It is interesting to note that while God revealed what would occur as far as which empires would rise up and eventually fall to one that came afterwards, it is also very clear that God Himself is ultimately in charge of bringing these things about. The better we understand that, the better off we'll be because we will have a more accurate picture of God's sovereignty over the affairs of humanity. Major events do not appear to be happenstance or accidents.

In fact, Daniel himself makes this clear in chapter two of Daniel. He unequivocally states, "*Let the name of God be blessed forever and ever, For wisdom and power belong to Him. It is He who changes the times and the epochs; He removes kings and establishes kings; He gives wisdom to wise men And knowledge to men of understanding. It is He who reveals the profound and hidden things; He knows what is in the darkness, And the light dwells with Him*" (Daniel 2:20-22).

This is something that we cannot remind ourselves of enough, can we? Either God is fully in charge or He is not at all in charge. History tends to prove that God is absolutely in charge and everyone who dies becomes very much aware of this fact. God is sovereign and it is terribly tragic that most people wait until after they have died and left this earth before they learn that truth.

The map below shows us that the Babylonian Empire was centered in the Middle East primarily. Of course, its headquarters was the capitol city of Babylon.

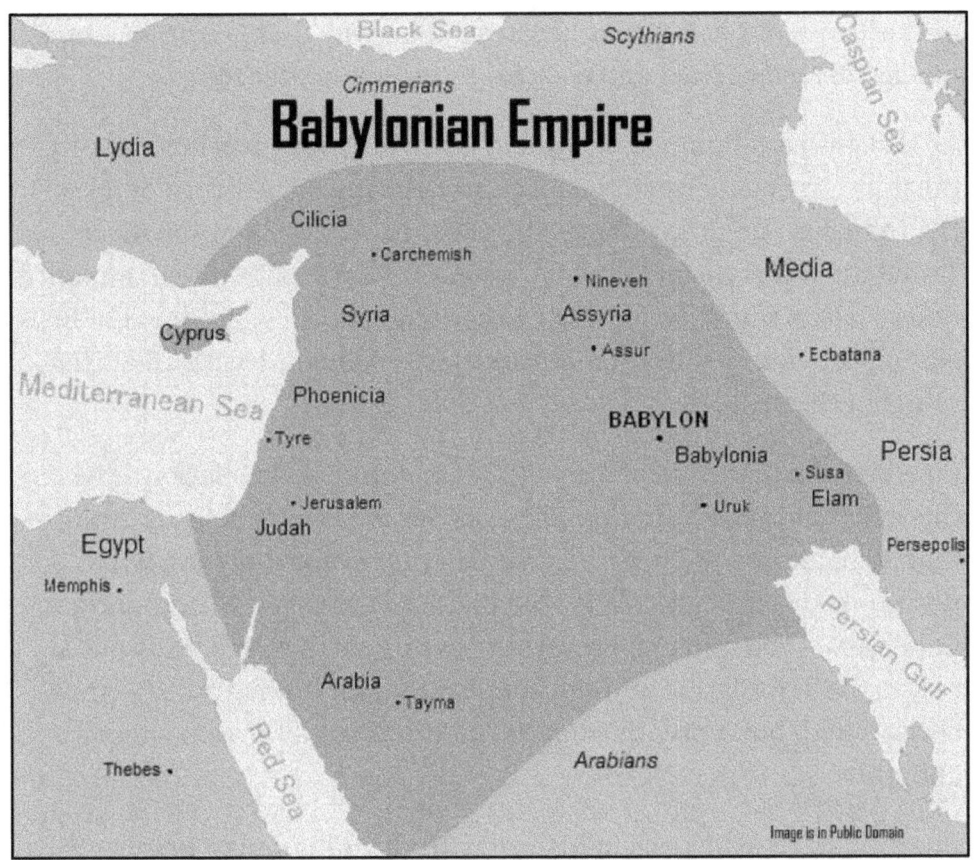

As can be seen from the map, the world looked then as it does today. Only the names and boundaries of empires and countries have changed. The geography has essentially remained the same.

What we will find as we go through the various empires that came into existence after Babylon is that they ultimately merged with the previous empire and usually expanded on that. Eventually, the new empire that replaced the previous one became larger, but had originally incorporated the area of the empire it conquered.

Prior to the Babylonian Kingdom – as mentioned previously – was Assyria, and prior to Assyria was Egypt. As also noted, though, God began His countdown where Israel was concerned with Nebuchadnezzar's kingdom of Babylon. This effectively began what is known as the Times of the Gentiles because of the way these Gentile nations would rule over Israel and trample Jerusalem under foot.

As is clear from Daniel 2, 7, 10, and elsewhere (such as Revelation), these empires take us all the way up to the physical return of Jesus. His return is not simply the event that ends the Tribulation/Great Tribulation. It is the event that also puts an end to Gentile dominance of Jerusalem. It will be fantastic to see, and of course the book of Revelation provides a vibrant picture of Jesus returning with all of His saints in His train.

Consider that truth for a moment. When John (in Revelation) saw this event unfold before his very eyes, we were part of Jesus' train, that is, all authentic Christians were in that event that John witnessed! Is this fantastic? The idea that John saw us – all authentic Christians – you and me – returning to this earth to see Jesus put a halt to the Tribulation and to vanquish the last human ruler – Antichrist – with but a breath from His mouth is something to shout about!

But it all starts way back in history with the Babylonian Empire. This is when Gentile rulers began to officially dominate and tread under foot Israel and especially Jerusalem where the Jewish Temple was erected.

Consider what this area of the world looks like today. The Temple Mount, though on paper fully owned by Israel, was left in the control of the Arabs after the Six-Day War of 1967. Israel didn't want to upset the apple cart so they allowed Arab control or oversight of the Temple Mount (and parts of East Jerusalem) to continue.

This was not an intelligent move because we can see how this has backfired on Israel today as most of the time, Jews are not allowed to go to the Temple Mount. Many are arrested for praying (moving their lips) and it is normally a very tense situation. Yet, God is in charge and His purposes will prevail.

Getting back to our empires, we see that as one empire fell, it really became part of the next empire. Can the same be said of Rome? *"The historical truth, if any exists, is that Rome did not fall; rather, it evolved. Roman coloni (farmers tied to the land) gradually became Medieval serfs. The patron-and-client relationship, so central in Roman society, slowly assumed the name and nature of the lord-and-vassal bond, the social order underlying much of European society in the Middle Ages. So, if Rome fell, it was only in slow motion, very slow motion."*[14]

Certainly, as we deal with the Roman Empire, we will consider the above statement and see if history proves it to be correct. From what we've seen at this point, we can say that one empire truly never disappears but is merely absorbed into the empire that replaces it in that same geographical area.

Remember the feet and toes of the statue Nebuchadnezzar saw in his dream (Daniel 2)? The legs represented the Roman Empire, but *below* the legs, there is another empire, or is it the same empire revived?

Prior to Jesus' physical return (represented by the Rock in the illustration that destroys the statue from the feet up), the feet and toes represent the final kingdom. Notice that when the Rock (aka Jesus) slams into the feet/toes, the entire statue is destroyed completely.

In referring to this Rock, Daniel 2:44b states that "it will crush and put an end to all these kingdoms, but it will itself endure forever." Jesus' return will completely obliterate not just the final kingdom, will "put an end to all these kingdoms." If each prior empire had truly

---

[14] http://www.usu.edu/markdamen/1320Hist&Civ/chapters/08ROMFAL.htm (3/19/2014)

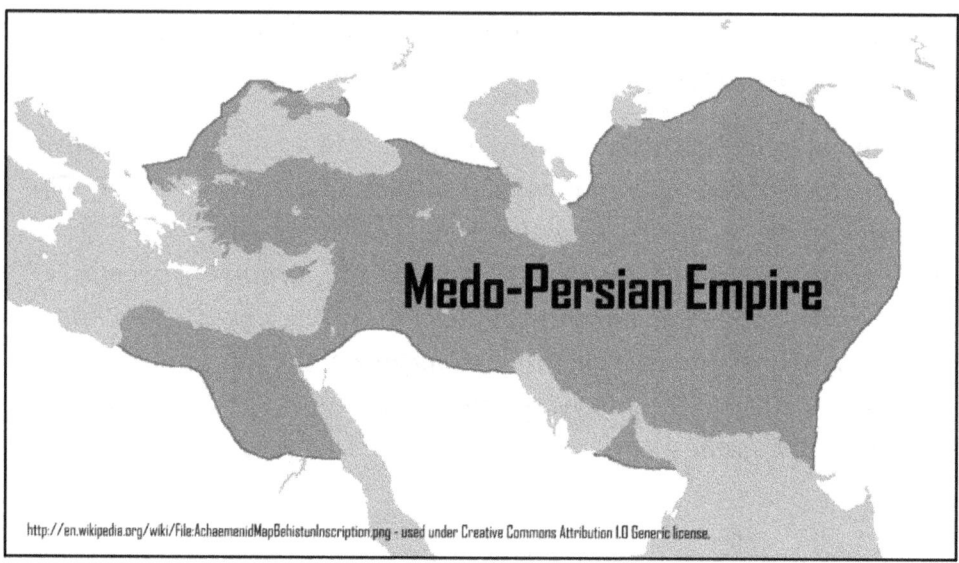

died, then Jesus would only actually be dealing with the last empire, which is the one that is in existence when He returns. However, the text implies that all the kingdoms were rolled into the one.

This final empire is different from all the rest and there is really one thing that makes it completely different from all the kingdoms that came before it.

We will get to that, but first, from the kingdom of Babylon, we segue to the kingdom of the Medes and Persians, or the Medo-Persian Empire.

The Medo-Persian Empire lasted from 539 BC to 331 BC, and rulership was through Darius for the Medes and Cyrus for the Persians. As we can readily see if we compare the geographical areas of the Babylonian, Median, and Persian Empires, they took up much of the same physical landmass, but simply grew larger and in different directions with each successive empire.

Of course, with respect to the Babylonian Empire being conquered by the Medo-Persian Empire, this makes sense if we understand, for instance, that Darius was literally waiting outside the city of Babylon while Belshazzar and his 1,000 guests dined and drank themselves into drunken stupors (cf. Daniel 5). Belshazzar was so confident that Babylon was impenetrable because of the huge wall that completely encircled the city, he felt he needn't worry about Darius and the Medes being positioned outside the wall.

Unfortunately for Belshazzar, it was time for his kingdom to be turned over to Darius. Because of that, God allowed Darius and his armies to block off the river that flowed into the city, cutting off the water supply. The armies were then able to enter the city through the dried-out river bed and they killed Belshazzar that very night. According to the Scripture we've already referenced, Darius was sixty-two years of age when he conquered Babylon and established the Median Empire.

If we consider our chart again, based on Daniel 2 and the statue that Nebuchadnezzar dreamed about, it is clear from Scripture that the Medes and the Persians are represented by the lopsided bear. This meant that though the two ruled together, the union of their two separate cultures never really happened.

Though the Medo-Persian Empire continued with Daniel living to become an old man (and Daniel being thrown in the lion's den occurred under Darius, in Daniel 6), when it was time, this empire was conquered by a young man who is seen as a leopard with four wings. So fast did Alexander the Great's kingdom rise and expand that he is exemplified first as a leopard with four wings and also as a male goat in Daniel 8.

This male goat is none other than Alexander the Great, and what is interesting is how his "horn" is broken into four sections. The following is from Daniel 8:5-8.

> *While I was observing, behold, a male goat was coming from the west over the surface of the whole earth without*

touching the ground; and the goat had a conspicuous horn between his eyes. He came up to the ram that had the two horns, which I had seen standing in front of the canal, and rushed at him in his mighty wrath. I saw him come beside the ram, and he was enraged at him; and he struck the ram and shattered his two horns, and the ram had no strength to withstand him. So he hurled him to the ground and trampled on him, and there was none to rescue the ram from his power. Then the male goat magnified himself exceedingly. But as soon as he was mighty, the large horn was broken; and in its place there came up four conspicuous horns toward the four winds of heaven.

Notice the last few sentences of the above quote. First, the male goat "magnified himself exceedingly." His ego was huge, and humanly speaking, we understand why. He managed to grow his empire so quickly and it became so vast that the previous empires paled in comparison. Second, he no sooner became "mighty" than his large "horn was broken."

The horn was broken into four pieces. This signifies the fact that when Alexander died at the age of 32, because he had no legitimate heir (his son had not yet been born), his empire was divided among his four generals (as noted).

Daniel 8:9-14 speaks of a "little horn" that came up out of one of the horns. Historically, this is a reference to Antiochus Epiphanes IV, who would have been under Seleucid's rule. Seleucid was the "king of the north," who, along with the king of the south, is referenced in another portion of the book of Daniel, chapter eleven.

More is also stated about Antiochus Epiphanes IV in Daniel 11:21-35. As it turns out, Antiochus ruled as the Seleucid king who reigned from 175-164 BC. *"Antiochus was the third son of Antiochus III the Great. After his father's defeat by the Romans in 190—189, he served as*

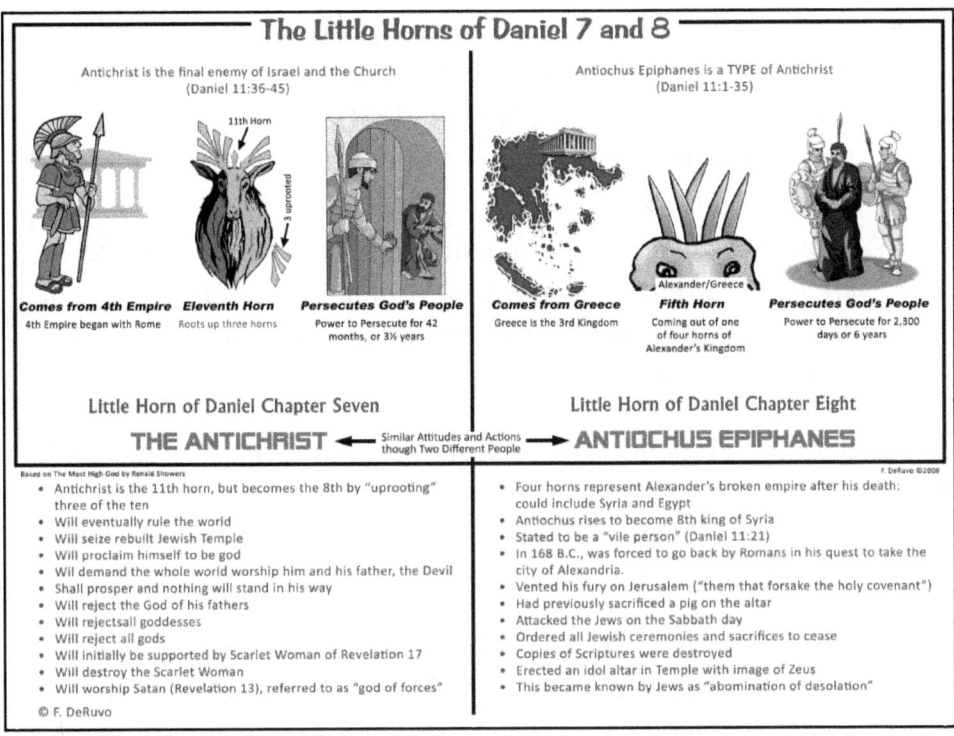

hostage for his father in Rome from 189 to 175, where he learned to admire Roman institutions and policies. His brother, King Seleucus IV, exchanged him for Demetrius, the son of Seleucus; and after Seleucus was murdered by Heliodorus, a usurper, Antiochus in turn ousted him."[15]

Antiochus was an interesting king. His rise to power was forecast in the book of Daniel in some detail. *"Antiochus' rise to power (Daniel 8; 11) corresponded to the following predictions by Daniel, the prophet of the Most High God:*

- *Antiochus would come to power after the untimely death of his predecessor.*

---

[15] "Antiochus IV Epiphanes," Britannica Corp, 2003

- *He was a contemptible person, thus he was called by many Antiochus Epiphanes (i.e., the madman) instead of his preferred appellation Epiphanes (i.e., God Manifest).*
- *He was not an heir to the throne, indeed to him 'royal majesty has not been given.'*
- *Antiochus did not lead a bloody coup, but he obtained "the kingdom by flatteries." Edward J. Young writes, "By flattery he won over the kings of Pergamus to his cause, and the Syrians gave in peaceably"*[16]

Antiochus was a devious man who wound up playing a rather notable part in history, which was something even Jesus referred to in His Olivet Discourse (Matthew 24) as the "abomination of desolation." This is detailed for us in Daniel 11:29-35 as well.

> *29 At the appointed time he will return and come into the South, but this last time it will not turn out the way it did before. 30 For ships of Kittim will come against him; therefore he will be disheartened and will return and become enraged at the holy covenant and take action; so he will come back and show regard for those who forsake the holy covenant. 31 Forces from him will arise, desecrate the sanctuary fortress, and do away with the regular sacrifice. And they will set up the abomination of desolation. 32 By smooth words he will turn to godlessness those who act wickedly toward the covenant, but the people who know their God will display strength and take action. 33 Those who have insight among the people will give understanding to the many; yet they will fall by sword and by flame, by captivity and by plunder for many days. 34 Now when they fall they will be granted a little help, and many will join with them in hypocrisy. 35 Some*

---

[16] https://www.christiancourier.com/articles/1191-daniels-prophecy-of-antiochus-epiphanes (3/19/2014)

*of those who have insight will fall, in order to refine,
purge and make them pure until the end time; because it
is still to come at the appointed time.*

The numerical references to individual verses have been left in for the above quote to make it easier to locate information. Notice verse 29 tells us that *"at the appointed time"* a person *"will return and come into the South...."* Unfortunately for this man (Antiochus IV), things don't turn out as he expects.

Antiochus will be successfully resisted (*"ships of Kittim will come against him"*) and he will fail in his military campaign. He will lose heart because of this and take out his anger and frustration on the Jews (*"the holy covenant"*).

The end of verse 30 tells us that he will *"show regard for those who forsake the holy covenant."* This means those Jews who turn their backs on God.

Verse 31 is very important. It states, *"forces from him will arise,"* and those forces would cause him to desecrate the sanctuary. This speaks of a man who was controlled by forces from within. Whatever those forces were – tremendous anger or hatred, or emotions due to demonic possession – they caused him to create the abomination that desolated. Those forces rose from within him. It's as if something triggered these other-worldly forces, prompting him to strike out at God Himself. He was merely using the Jews and the Jewish Temple to accomplish that act.

This type of behavior is supremely demonic. It is something that Satan would do because of his abject hatred for God. Satan knows he has lost. He knows he has his role to play and he knows what his end will be. That final destiny that makes him an eternal guest in the Lake of Fire does not sit well with him. His hatred grows because of it and I'm sure he goes back and forth from believing that he will overcome and overthrow God to knowing that he doesn't have a sliver of a chance to accomplish that very thing he craves.

Here in history, he used Antiochus IV to inflict physical terror on the Jews of that day. He used a man to desecrate the Temple, and from that man he struck out at God's chosen people.

According to history, when Antiochus IV, on his way back from military defeat, went into the Jewish Temple, he slaughtered a pig on the altar. He went so far as to sprinkle the blood around the Holy Place and some historians even tell us that he set up a statue of Zeus there, possibly with or without a mask of his own face over Zeus' face.

The remainder of the quoted verses establish the fact that tremendous persecution would occur and indeed did occur after this terrible desecration of God's Temple. In essence, Antiochus is a *"small horn"* who would typify the final *"man of sin"* (2 Thessalonians 2:3), as he is called by Paul.

The *"man of sin,"* or Antichrist, who comes at the end of this age and who rises to supreme power in the coming Revised Roman Empire will act as Antiochus IV acted, but with greater supernatural power, far greater hatred, and an all-consuming desire to magnify himself above God.

Antichrist will be his spiritual father's son. He will be fully empowered and possessed by Satan himself. I believe that God brought about the situations of the past as seen in Antiochus IV and other tyrants in order for us to know what the Antichrist would also accomplish.

One day, when the final empire has taken complete shape, and the ten horns of Daniel and Revelation are ruling the world's global empire, another *"horn"* will rise up among them and take his preordained place in future history. There, he will blaspheme the holy

Name of God Almighty, do the works of Satan as no one has done them before, and seek to honor only himself.

Persecution will be like nothing this world has ever seen before. At the same time, God's wrath will be poured out on humanity through the seals, trumpets, and bowl judgments outlined in the book of Revelation. It will be a terrible time for the people on this earth then.

If we think it is getting bad now (and it is), one can only imagine what it will be like when the entire world is under full control of a man totally empowered, corrupted, and possessed by Satan. It is difficult to imagine, yet it is coming.

Chapter 7
More About the Roman Empire

As we mentioned in the first part of this book, the Roman Empire began inauspiciously enough. Rome was not built in a day (and neither was any other empire, including the present European Union). It took time for the greatest empire known in history to arrive to its zenith, but it did arrive.

Nigel Rodgers, in his book titled *Roman Empire*, referred to Rome as the first "*superpower.*" Certainly, this is a true statement.

"The Roman Empire was the resolution of the seven-hundred-year struggle of various social classes and competing political systems. Ro-

man history recounts the gradual triumph of democracy and popular government over an exclusive governing caste."[17]

As one might expect, the process was long and arduous, but eventually, mighty Rome, which began as a city on seven hills, transformed itself into the greatest human empire that has yet existed. In fact, its eventual size is one of the reasons for Rome's eventual fall.

As can be seen from the map, the Roman Empire included pretty much all the geographic land that previous empires were made of and added to it. It took over more of Northern Africa and had a far greater reach into Europe, including Great Britain.

The empire also pushed further east as well as south. Mighty Rome had become larger than any previous empire and felt strong and confident because of it.

Of course, like the empires that existed previously, Rome rose or fell at God's command, not Caesar's. Eventually, as we know, after Rome

---

[17] *The International Standard Bible Encyclopedia*, Vol. Four Q-Z (1988), p. 208

had reached its zenith, the decline began, due not necessarily to the killing of Jesus, but because of Rome's part in its attack of the Holy City Jerusalem in AD 70. This was the beginning of the end, in a biblical sense.

However, prior to this major event, which turned catastrophic for the Roman Empire, Rome first allowed the persecution of Christians. This did not happen immediately either during the physical life of Jesus or immediately upon His death (resurrection, and ascension).

Persecution of Christians began over a period of time. Tiberius had reigned during the time of Christ, but he died in AD 37, which was ultimately too early to form any real opinion about Christianity since in many ways, it was still considered to be part of Judaism.

This was still the case when the next emperor Gaius reigned (from AD 37 – 41). During Gaius' reign, he inadvertently took the attention off of Christians because of his direct persecution of Jews. It's almost as if Claudius, the next emperor (AD 41 – 45) took the baton from Gaius, continuing the persecution.

It was not until the reign of Nero (AD 54 – 68) that all Roman eyes turned toward Christians. Specifically, it was after the fire in AD 64, in which Nero likely started a fire that destroyed much of Rome, that things turned hostile toward Christians. They were made the scapegoat for the fire that he had likely ordered to be started.

Christians after this were arrested (if they admitted to being Christians) and were charged with hatred of mankind. *"The victims perished amid mockery; some clothed in the skins of wild beasts were torn to pieces by dogs...Whence (after these cruelties) commiseration began to be felt for them, though guilty and deserving the severest penalties, for men felt their destruction was not from considerations of public welfare but to gratify the cruelty of one person (Nero)."*[18]

Eventually, it was felt that Christians were undermining the religion of the state and *"earned the hatred of the populace, and a sect so detested must have fallen under surveillance of the city police administration. They were chosen by Nero as scapegoats to serve his purposes. The origin of the first persecution was thus purely accidental – in order to remove suspicion from the emperor."*[19]

Nothing remains unchanged in life. Eventually, persecution died down, but it took a while. In fact, it took several emperors before persecution of Christians began to wane. It wasn't until after the death of Domitian that *"peace prevailed for the Christians during the reign of Nerva and the first thirteen years of Trajan."*[20]

However, this peace did not prevail forever, as we know. Various emperors after Nerva either tolerated Christians or hated them. But God used this period to force Christians to flee throughout the Roman Empire where the Gospel could be preached as well. Because of persecution, Christianity grew throughout the empire, changing lives for eternity wherever the Gospel was preached.

During the period of AD 192 – 284, Christianity's spread occurred virtually unmolested. The primary reason has to do with the fact that in the space of these 92 years, Rome experienced 20 emperors. No one ruler really stayed around long enough to focus on Christianity and time had long passed since Nero's bid to blame Christians for the fire that had destroyed a good portion of Rome.

Finally, in AD 313, through Constantine (AD 311 – 476), came the first general edict of toleration regarding Christianity. The edict was

---

[18] *The International Standard Bible Encyclopedia*, Vol. Four Q-Z (1988), p. 216
[19] Ibid
[20] Ibid, p. 217

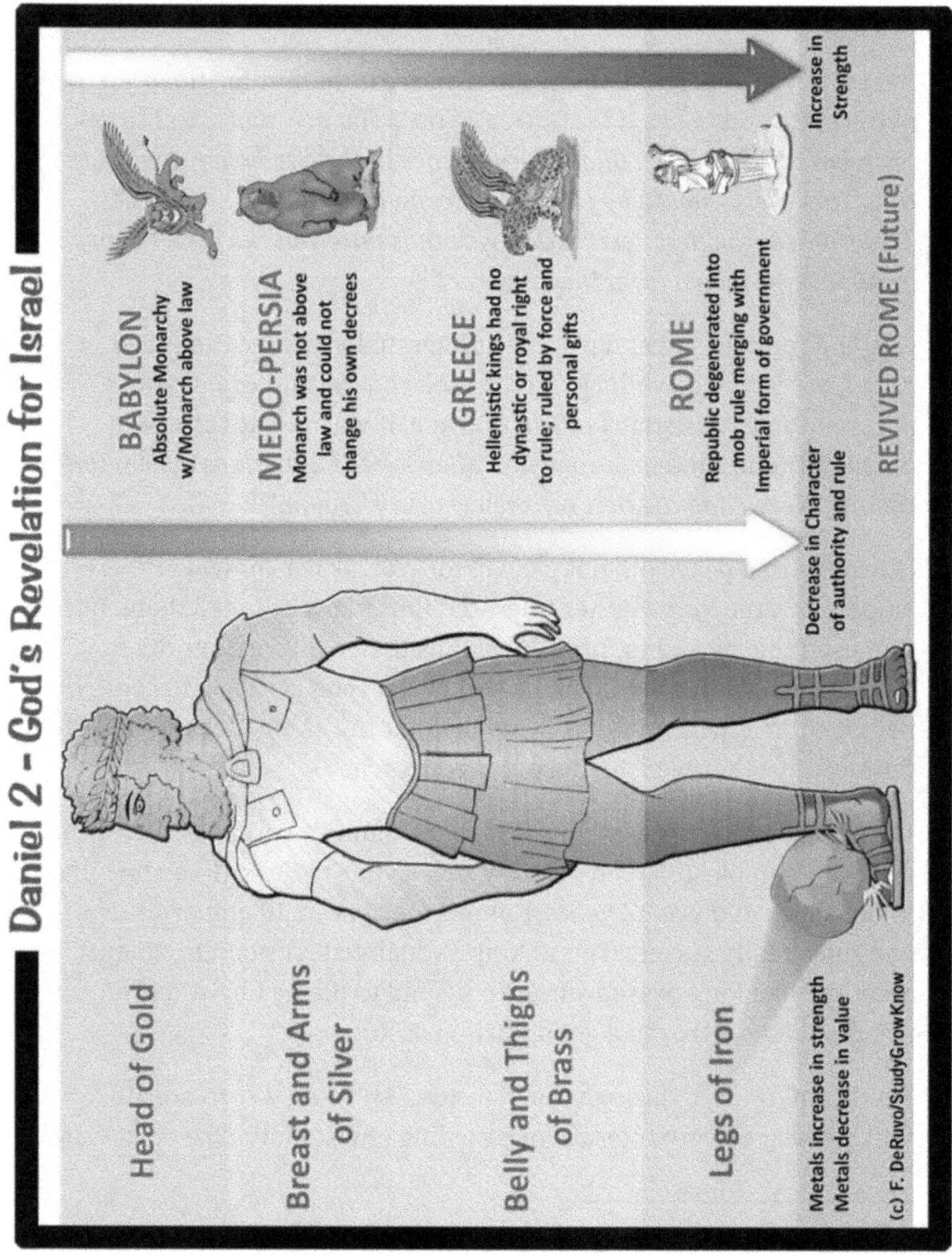

issued from the city of Milan, Italy and this caused Christianity to be seen as equal to the paganism that reigned throughout the empire.

In truth, this persecution of Christians and the destruction of Jerusalem and the Jewish Temple were the very things that started the downhill slide for Rome. At the same time, please note that from Daniel 2 we learn that the two legs of the statue – the Roman Empire – lead directly to the two feet. In fact, please remember that everything is connected to what comes afterwards, starting with the head. It is most likely why God used the image of the statue as He did in Nebuchadnezzar's dream. The concept of the human body and how it functions is very important here.

Refer to the illustration that we have reprinted on the opposite page of the statue that Nebuchadnezzar dreamed about. The head made of gold sits on top of the body, connected to the neck/shoulder area. But in the image, the head itself is made of gold, signifying superior value to everything that comes after it.

The chest and arms are made of silver and the two arms represent the fact that there are two cultures in that empire, the Medes and the Persians. The next empire down (to come after the Medo-Persian Empire) is the Grecian Empire, led by Alexander the Great. His kingdom is made of brass and that kingdom leads into the great Roman Empire. The two legs represent the final stages of the empire, when it was divided into a western and an eastern branch.

But also notice that the feet are considered to be a separate (and final) Gentile kingdom. This kingdom is still part of the legs, just as our feet and legs connect. What this means is that the feet are of the same type as the legs, but are also different.

If we stop to consider and compare, we will note that each successive kingdom, signified by a specific metal, increases in strength, but decreases in value. Gold is more valuable than any of the other metals noted on the statue. At the same time, gold is not as strong as silver and certainly not as strong as iron.

God chose these images and symbols specifically. The Roman Empire was certainly the strongest of all these empires, yet it was the least valuable as far as worth is concerned. But its strength is what is keeping the Roman Empire alive today. Yes, it is alive today, but not as the Roman Empire. It is alive as something else entirely.

It was in AD 290 that *"Emperor Diocletian decided to shift the center of the Roman Empire to the east. The new state was known as the Byzantine, or Eastern Roman Empire. Then the western half divided into 5 parts split up among the Germanic tribes who continued to carry the mantle of Rome. The German rulers saw themselves as heirs of Rome."*[21]

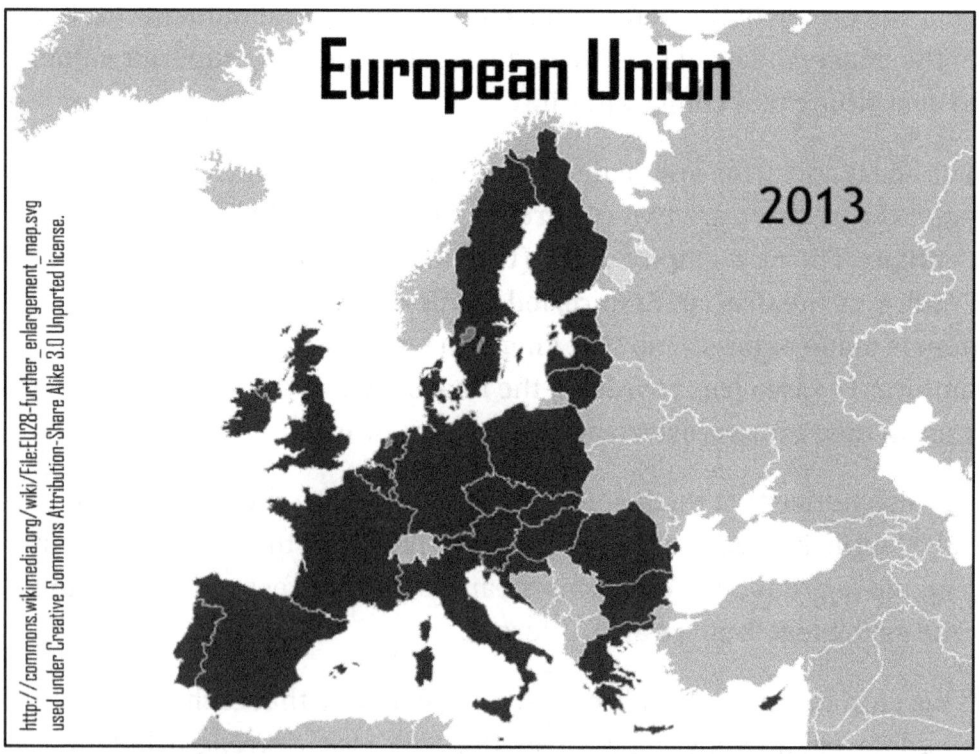

---

[21] http://focusonjerusalem.com/theidentityofthe7.html (3/19/2014)

As Rome continued, eventually Charlemagne became ruler and *"unified Western Europe [and] recreated an equivalent of the old Roman Empire."*[22] Pope Leo III had crowned him legal heir to the previous western emperors.

Charlemagne became the emperor of the Roman Empire and this title eventually changed into "Holy Roman Emperor" until 1806. The western "leg" of the empire became known as the Holy Roman Empire.

If we look at Europe today, we see an entity known as the European Union (EU). There are 28 individual countries in the EU, but 5 of them – Spain, Britain, France, Italy, and Germany – were also part of the old Roman Empire.

When the EU was in its infancy, only Belgium, Germany, France, Italy, Luxembourg and the Netherlands cooperated with one another economically, and that was in 1951-52. The concept for the EU has been around for many years and has grown quite a bit since then.

The following countries are now part of the EU (followed by date they entered the EU)[23]:

- Austria   1995
- Belgium   1952 (founding member)
- Bulgaria   2007
- Croatia   2013
- Cyprus   2004
- Czech Republic   2004
- Denmark   1973
- Estonia   2004
- Finland   1995
- France*   1952 (founding member)

---

[22] http://focusonjerusalem.com/theidentityofthe7.html (3/19/2014)
[23] http://europa.eu/about-eu/countries/member-countries/ (3/21/2014)

- Germany*   1952 (founding member)
- Greece   1981
- Hungary   2004
- Ireland   1973
- Italy*   1952 (founding member)
- Latvia   2004
- Lithuania   2004
- Luxembourg   1952 (founding member)
- Malta   2004
- Netherlands   1952 (founding member)
- Poland   2004
- Portugal   1986
- Romania   2007
- Slovakia   2004
- Slovenia   2004
- Spain*   1986
- Sweden   1995
- United Kingdom* 1973

The previous list of nations also highlights countries that have the largest voting blocs (those with an *asterisk*[24]). The small map included in this chapter shows where the EU is geographically in the world. As can be seen, many of the countries that are part of this union of countries were part of the old Roman Empire.

It's also interesting to note that many of the countries that are part of the EU are now (and have been) experiencing tremendous problems due to the incursion of Muslims over the decades. In countries like the Netherlands and the United Kingdom, the Islamic population has increased drastically, giving Muslims there tremendous power. This power is creating major problems due to the growing demands of

---

[24] http://en.wikipedia.org/wiki/Voting_in_the_Council_of_the_European_Union (3/23/2014)

Muslims and government leaders who are willing to go along with these demands.

The face of many of these nations is changing radically, creating upheaval and civil unrest. Too often, Muslims who commit crimes are given slaps on the wrist or very light sentences compared to the indigenous population. This is adding fuel to the fire.

But if the EU is picking up where the western leg of the Roman Empire left off, what, if anything, picked up where the eastern leg left off?

Now, what about the eastern leg of the old Roman Empire? Does that still exist in some form or another? Well, obviously, the geography remains, doesn't it? That never goes away, but it's important to find out what, if anything, took over the eastern leg of the old Roman Empire, and if something did, what was it? Beyond this, is that empire or kingdom still with us today, and if so, will it play any part in ushering in the final "beast" of Daniel and Revelation?

Clearly, if the eastern leg of the old Roman Empire was swallowed by something else, then it also makes sense that it segued into something else as well. Together, the EU and this other "kingdom" form the two feet of King Nebuchadnezzar's statue, or at least the ankles of the two feet. The feet themselves will form the basis for the final Gentile empire, the very one that will be utterly destroyed (along with everything that came before it) when Jesus physically returns. Surely, that's worth an "amen."

Chapter 8
Ottoman Turkish Rule

The Ottoman Empire (or "House of Osman") grew out of the eastern leg of the Roman Empire, but by this time was called the Byzantine Empire and was headed by Constantine. *"The origins of the great civilization known as the Byzantine Empire can be traced to 330 A.D., when the Roman emperor Constantine I dedicated a 'new Rome' on the site of the ancient Greek colony of Byzantium."*[25] The ancient city of Byzantium had been *"founded by Greek colonists from Megara around 657."*[26]

In many ways, the *"Byzantine Empire was the successor of the Roman Empire in the Greek-speaking, eastern part of the Mediterranean. Christian in nature,* **it was perennially at war with the Muslims**[.]

---

[25] http://www.history.com/topics/ancient-history/byzantine-empire (3/23/2014)
[26] Ibid.

Flourishing during the reign of the Macedonian emperors, its demise was the consequence of attacks by Seljuk Turks, Crusaders, and Ottoman Turks."[27]

Emphasis has been added to the above quote, noting that Muslims became a thorn in the flesh to every nation or culture that was not Islamic. This tension often broke out in wars and skirmishes that eventually gave rise to the Ottoman Empire.

Ultimately, the Byzantine Empire fell to the growing Ottoman Empire in 1453 with the capture of Constantinople. Artillery actually made the difference in allowing the Ottoman Turks to overcome Constantinople, which at that time was the headquarters for Christianity.

Of course, in between AD 330 and 1453, the eastern part of the Roman Empire (or "new Rome" in Byzantium) went through growth cycles of its own. The Germanic tribes of the Goths, Visigoths, Ostrogoths, and Vandals had begun chipping away at the outer edges of the Roman Empire. There were victories and losses until eventually the Muslims chased the Byzantines out of Levant (modern-day Tur-

---

[27] http://www.ancient.eu.com/Byzantine_Empire/ (3/23/2014)

key, Syria, and Lebanon).

By the early AD 1000s, Byzantine was in decline, and the monarchs that ruled the empire were unable to completely contain or manage the empire. Finally, in 1453, the Ottoman Empire conquered Constantinople, taking over its government.

Due to the decline of cultural life there, many artists and scholars fled to Italy and other areas, taking with them valuable manuscripts. In essence, the *"Ottoman Empire [was] empire created by Turkish tribes in Anatolia. One of the most powerful states in the world during the 15th and 16th centuries, it spanned more than 600 years and came to an end only in 1922, when it was replaced by the Turkish Republic and various successor states in southeastern Europe and the Middle East.*[28]

The Ottoman flag is bright red with a crescent moon and one star. Flags that Islamic countries use today often have the same motif.

As can be seen on the map of the Ottoman Empire, historians believed it to have had its beginnings in approximately AD 1300 and its official end in 1922. This length represents many changes and leaders, but in the end, it had a long run.

The beginnings of the Ottoman Empire ran side-by-side with the old Byzantine Empire. It was not until 1453 that Constantinople was conquered under Mehmed II.

During the period from 1908 – 1922, the Ottoman Empire began its decline and eventual defeat. Turkish in origin, the Ottoman Empire represented the largest Islamic empire in history.

---

[28] http://www.britannica.com/EBchecked/topic/434996/Ottoman-Empire (3/23/2014)

Today, Muslims will note that under the caliphate of the Ottoman Empire, non-Muslims were often treated as secondary citizens, especially if they were Christians or Jews. *"In the Ottoman Empire, in accordance with the Muslim dhimmi system, Christians were guaranteed limited freedoms (such as the right to worship), but were treated as second-class citizens. Christians and Jews were not considered equals to Muslims: testimony against Muslims by Christians and Jews was inadmissible in courts of law. They were forbidden to carry weapons or ride atop horses, their houses could not overlook those of Muslims, and their religious practices would have to defer to those of Muslims, in addition to various other legal limitations."*[29]

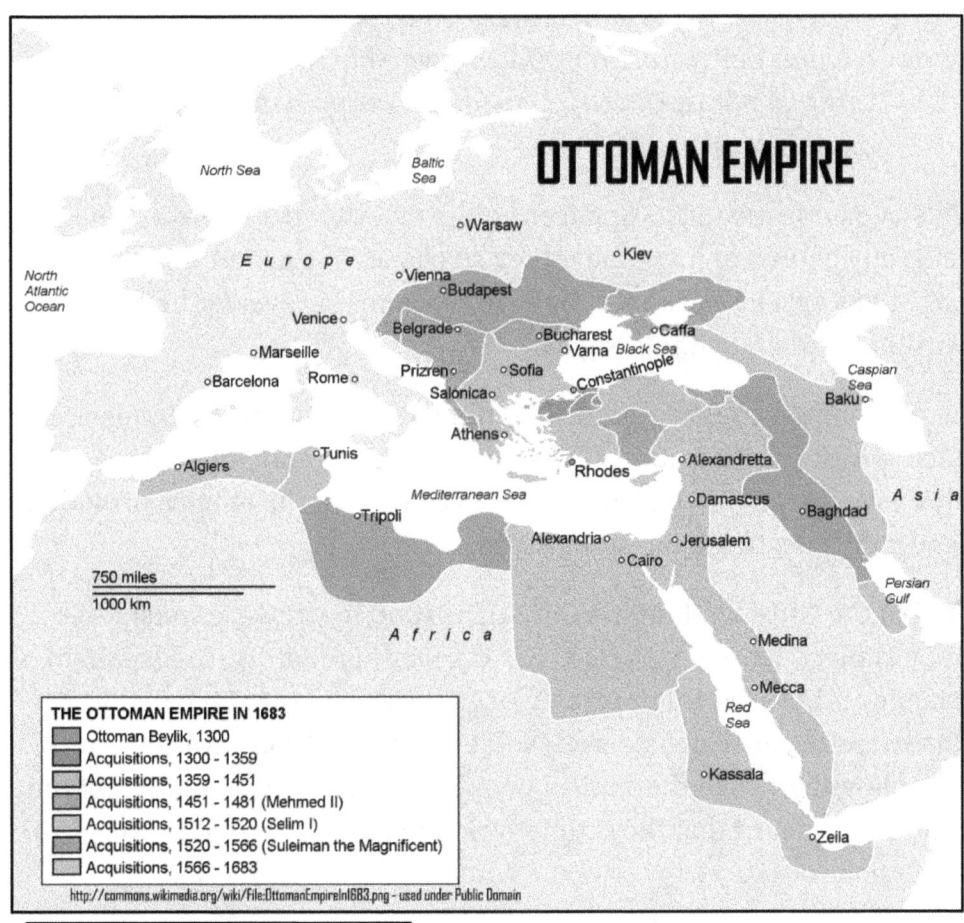

[29] http://en.wikipedia.org/wiki/Ottoman_Empire (3/25/2014)

A "dhimmi" in the Islamic legal system is someone who is "protected" or "guilty," depending upon how the Arabic word is used. As author Robert Spencer notes, Christians and Jews are "protected" because of the revelations it is believed we have received from God, but "guilty" because we have rejected Muhammad.

This puts the Jew and Christian at a lower status than the Muslim and *"was first articulated by Umar ibn al-Khattab, who was caliph from 634 to 644. According to the Qur'anic commentary of Ibn Kathir, the Christians making this pact with Umar pledged:*

> *'We made a condition on ourselves that we will neither erect in our areas a monastery, church, or a sanctuary for a monk, nor restore any place of worship that needs restoration nor use any of them for the purpose of enmity against Muslims.'"*[30]

This of course meant, as Spencer points out, that the Muslims could seize any church at any time if they so chose. The conditions that Christians agreed to essentially placed them at a level far below the Muslim, virtually without rights.

Aside from a secondary stature within Islam, "dhimmi" also references a system of taxation. Christians and Jews (and other "undesirables") were allowed to remain (and even live) in the empire provided they paid a tax to Islamic authorities.

Within the Ottoman Empire, Christians (and Jews) were considered to be subject people, and as such, a tax was mandatory, to be paid to Islamic authorities. But it wasn't just a tax that was to be paid by Christians or those considered "subject" people. There were many other laws by which the subject people must live. Any violation of the conditions meant that they could be killed or could be made to become slaves.

---

[30] Robert Spencer, *The Politically Incorrect Guide to Islam* (2005), p. 49

This same attitude exists today within countries and even areas controlled by Islam. In Egypt, there have been numerous reports and articles about how Muslims have gone rampaging through one area to another, burning churches to the ground. On some occasions, the churches were filled with worshipers.[31] [32] One article individually lists the specific churches that were destroyed by the Muslim Brotherhood.[33]

Many within Islam (or outside of Islam who are apologists for Islam) will tell you that Jews had better experiences while in Muslim lands than in other parts of Europe considered Christian areas. That is simply not true.

Robert Spencer points out the origins of this myth:

> *PC spokesmen assert every day that even if the dhimma really did subject Jews and Christians to ongoing and institutionalized discrimination and harassment, it certainly wasn't as bad as the way Jews were treated in Christian Europe. Historian Paul Johnson explains: 'In theory...the status of the Jewish dhimmi under Moslem rule was worse than under the Christians, since their right to practice their religion, and even their right to live, might be arbitrarily removed at any time. In practice, however, the Arab warriors who conquered half the civilized world so rapidly in the seventh and eighth centuries had no wish to exterminate literate and industrious Jewish communities who provided them with reliable tax incomes and served them in innumerable ways'.*[34]

---

[31] http://www.foxnews.com/world/2013/08/19/muslim-brotherhood-wages-war-on-christians/ (3/25/2014)
[32] http://www.speroforum.com/a/PQZVKGJNIZ10/74237-Muslims-burn-47-churches-in-Egypt#.UzGi8vldV8E (3/25/2014)
[33] http://patdollard.com/2013/08/egypt-list-of-churches-that-have-been-destroyed-by-muslim-brotherhood-supporters/ (3/25/2014)
[34] Robert Spencer, *The Politically Incorrect Guide to Islam* (2005), p. 57

The real tragedy here – aside from lives lost – is that many continue to believe that Islam is a religion of peace, yet how can this be when there is so much violence and brutality associated with Islam? Either it is peaceful or it isn't, but it cannot be both.

One of the things that it seems necessary to point to is not the actual religion itself (because people will point to the Crusades as an example of the bad things that were done in the name of Christianity), but instead, it is the founders that should be highlighted. When we look to Jesus, we learn what type of person He was as He lived among people on this earth. We do the same thing with Muhammad and then we are able to compare those two founders to one another. From there, we can rightly make a decision about who was the more peaceful individual.

Taking this tact with people can generally help them peel back the layers of each religion. However, some individuals refuse to approach the subject honestly, preferring to stick with people who call themselves Christian and not dealing with the reality of the founders.

When I ran an article written with this approach on my blog page[35] and highlighted it through Twitter, I was almost immediately attacked by a Muslim who felt I was filled with bigotry and simply publishing the article as a form of disinformation. The problem for that person, though, was that the article contained factual information about Muhammad that portrayed him as a warrior.

Jesus did not carry a sword. He never physically retaliated when someone got physical with Him. He never killed anyone. In fact, Jesus never married and certainly never had sexual relations outside of marriage.

---

[35] http://www.studygrowknowblog.com

Mohammed VI, Sultan of Turkey, 1861-1926, the last caliph of the Ottoman Empire. (Image from Library of Congress)

Muhammad carried a sword. He robbed caravans and later with his followers slaughtered villages of people. He "married" a young girl of nine by the name of Aisha. He had many wives.

When people are faced with this information, the first thing they will say is, "what about King David?" or they will point to someone else in the Bible. But they are missing the point. Deliberately comparing Jesus with Muhammad is the point because both of these individuals founded a religion. King David did not found a religion. He was simply a servant of the Most High God.

Based on the actuality of the two founders, who was more peaceful, Jesus or Muhammad? If Muhammad carried a sword, robbed, and killed people (especially those considered to be infidels, or non-Muslims), then who would be the better Muslim today? Would that person be the one who is "peaceful" and gets along with people or the one who also does what Muhammad did? The answer should be clear if people are honest. The person who most emulates Muhammad is the Muslim who lives as Muhammad lived. It's really a no-brainer, yet people still debate and attempt to rewrite history and redefine Muhammad.

There is a great deal of money being spent by Islamic factions to whitewash history. They want people to believe that Islam truly is a religion of peace, yet there are too many examples today of the fact that Islam is not a religion of peace. At the very least, it can be said that not all Muslims have received the memo about how peaceful Islam is supposed to be.

We need look no further than Great Britain, France, The Netherlands, and many other parts of Europe and Asia. There is tremendous turmoil there because Muslims, rather than adopting aspects of the culture of their adopted country, demand that they be given special status that allows them to ignore and avoid laws. It becomes absolutely absurd trying to meet the constant demands of Islam in a civilized world.

This is why – in large part – the toes are iron mixed with clay. These two materials do not mix. There is no way they can mix. You can cover an iron pillar in clay to carve a design in it. It will hide the iron underneath and make the outside of a structure look nice and decorative. However, that is not the same as mixing the two substances. Iron is iron and clay is clay. The two cannot be mixed.

Such is Islam. It has a will of iron and simply refuses to mix with clay. In fact, it cannot mix with anything else because of its nature. This was clearly seen during parts of the Ottoman Empire and it continues today as Islam itself continues. The end of the Ottoman Empire did not spell the end for Islam. In fact, Islam does just fine without its own country.

Today, Islam is moving stalwartly toward another caliphate. Their militancy is apparent on every level. They wish to rule the world again and they believe that they will have that opportunity.

We have more to cover, and beginning with our next chapter we will look more intently at Daniel 2, followed by Daniel 7. We will then move on to Revelation 13 and Revelation 17.

It is very important to understand all of the symbolism used in Scripture. All of it points to something specific and means only one thing. When you're done reading this book, it is our hope that you will have a great understanding of exactly what these chapters mean and what they mean for today.

Are we living in the time that Daniel saw hundreds of years ago? I believe we are, and because of that, Daniel's visions are more important for us than they were then. That is not to minimize the impact of Scripture on Daniel's life. It is to emphasize that Daniel was told to seal up the vision until such a time when the visions were applicable (cf. Daniel 12). That would be toward the end of the age in which we are living.

Chapter 9
Daniel 2 Revisited

Daniel 2 is the first chapter in which we learn about Nebuchadnezzar's dream that robbed him of sleep. As we noted, it included the image of a very large statue made up of various materials, each section of the image representing a different empire or kingdom.

Ultimately, through God's revelation to Daniel, we learned what the dream was and what it meant. We also noted that beginning with Nebuchadnezzar's kingdom of Babylon, something called the Times of the Gentiles had begun. Paul alludes to this in Romans 11:25 as he notes another aspect of this period of time, when the emphasis will not be on Israel, but on what God is doing through Gentiles and calling them to become part of His Church.

Several passages in the Hebrew Bible (the Old Testament) are marked out because they also allude to this time period. Besides this Daniel 2 passage, Ezekiel 30:2b-3 seems to align with it.

> *Wail, 'Alas for the day!'*
> *For the day is near,*
> *Even the day of the Lord is near;*
> *It will be a day of clouds,*
> *A time of doom for the nations.*

Jesus also references the conclusion of this period of time in His Olivet Discourse (Matthew 24, Mark 13, and Luke 21). This time is a very important time in God's timetable.

But Daniel 2 is the chapter that provides details and clues that we need to address and understand. In doing so, we will have a greater grasp of God's plan of redemption and how things are moving as we approach the end of the age, just prior to the time of Jesus' physical return.

We've gone over some of Daniel 2, but there are a few more things we should take the time to consider. Verses 31 to 35 provide a summary of the entire dream as given to Daniel.

> *You, O king, were looking and behold, there was a single great statue; that statue, which was large and of extraordinary splendor, was standing in front of you, and its appearance was awesome. The head of that statue was made of fine gold, its breast and its arms of silver, its belly and its thighs of bronze, its legs of iron, its feet partly of iron and partly of clay. You continued looking until a stone was cut out without hands, and it struck the statue on its feet of iron and clay and crushed them. Then the*

iron, the clay, the bronze, the silver and the gold were crushed all at the same time and became like chaff from the summer threshing floors; and the wind carried them away so that not a trace of them was found. But the stone that struck the statue became a great mountain and filled the whole earth.

Again, we see the statue and the order in which the materials change going from the top to the bottom. There is gold, silver, bronze, iron, and finally iron mixed with clay with respect to the feet.

As we have noted, each new material represents a different empire. Gold represents Babylon, silver is Medo-Persia, bronze is Alexander's Grecian Empire, and iron (down to and including the iron mixed with clay) is the Roman Empire.

Please notice that the stone cut without hands completely crushes everything that came before it when it hits the feet of the statue. Not only that, but it fills the whole earth, meaning it becomes a global kingdom.

The stone, of course, represents the Messianic Kingdom of Jesus, who will physically reign for 1,000 years following the Tribulation/Great Tribulation. His Kingdom will utterly destroy every manmade kingdom that came before Him. There will be nothing left, and the fact that these previous kingdoms become like chaff and are carried away by the wind so that not even the smallest trace is left tells us that there will be no remembrance of them. All eyes will be on Jesus at that point.

Daniel 2 provides us with a brief summary of the kingdoms, what they are, their "value" and their "strength." Note that the metals decrease in value going from the top of the statue down to the feet and they also increase in strength going from the head to the feet. This is why when we come to the Roman Empire (legs of iron and feet of iron and clay), there is tremendous strength (or staying power) in that fourth empire, but not much value in the material itself when compared to the head of gold.

This is partly why the fourth beast – the Roman Empire – is so terrifying to Daniel, as we'll see in upcoming verses. Once Daniel tells the king what his dream consisted of, he then provides the interpretation for him (and us):

> *This was the dream; now we will tell its interpretation before the king. You, O king, are the king of kings, to whom the God of heaven has given the kingdom, the power, the strength and the glory; and wherever the sons of men dwell, or the beasts of the field, or the birds of the sky, He has given them into your hand and has caused you to rule over them all. You are the head of gold.* (Daniel 2:36-38)

Daniel affirms to King Nebuchadnezzar that he (or his kingdom) is represented by the head of gold. That is our starting point and it cannot be disputed.

Notice Daniel tells Nebuchadnezzar that he was given the kingdom, the power, the strength, and the glory obviously by God Himself. Nebuchadnezzar also had the power and ability to expand his kingdom to whatever size he wanted (wherever the sons of men dwell), but apparently didn't choose to do that.

Nebuchadnezzar was specifically chosen by God to rule at that period of time and have the kingdom that God gave him. This of course confirms to us that God Himself sets up and removes people who are in positions of authority and rulership. It also should prove to us that God sets up kings and rulers who are evil as well. At the very least, we can say that God allows these individuals to rule and He does so for His unique purposes. We can assume from this and other areas of Scripture that God is in charge, period.

This is not to say that Nebuchadnezzar was evil (though it's clear he had a temper and understood his authority to take life or give it). We need to remember, though, that at first, Nebuchadnezzar did not recognize the authority of Daniel's God and still viewed himself as being a type of god. Eventually, God shows Nebuchadnezzar who is in charge and Nebuchadnezzar is humbled and becomes a better king because of it.

Daniel 2:39 is short and to the point, but more detail is provided in other sections of Scripture.

> *After you there will arise another kingdom inferior to you, then another third kingdom of bronze, which will rule over all the earth.*

Historically, we know that the next kingdom to come into existence following the Babylonian Empire was the Medo-Persian Empire, headed by Cyrus and Darius. Though Daniel does not say it here, this kingdom is represented by silver and is inferior to Babylon.

The kingdom after that (the third kingdom) is ruled by Alexander the Great of Greece. His kingdom, as represented by bronze, is also less valuable, and therefore inferior to Nebuchadnezzar's.

The very next empire introduced (the fourth) turns out to be the Roman Empire, and Daniel spends a bit more time detailing this kingdom in verses 40 through 43.

> *Then there will be a fourth kingdom as strong as iron; inasmuch as iron crushes and shatters all things, so, like iron that breaks in pieces, it will crush and break all these in pieces. In that you saw the feet and toes, partly of potter's clay and partly of iron, it will be a divided kingdom; but it will have in it the toughness of iron, inasmuch as you saw the iron mixed with common clay. As the toes of the feet were partly of iron and partly of pottery, so some*

> *of the kingdom will be strong and part of it will be brittle.*
> *And in that you saw the iron mixed with common clay,*
> *they will combine with one another in the seed of men;*
> *but they will not adhere to one another, even as iron does*
> *not combine with pottery.*

Again, Rome is likened to iron here, at least at the start. As we travel down the legs of the statue, which meet the feet, the iron becomes "mixed" with clay. However, as we have noted, these two substances do not mix.

Dr. Thomas Constable notes, "*The final form of the fourth kingdom—Daniel did not identify it as a fifth kingdom—would not have the cohesiveness that the earlier kingdoms possessed.*"[36]

This is also how the kingdom is classified just prior to the physical return of Jesus Christ. Daniel says that it is a "divided" kingdom. That division began with the separation of the Roman Empire into the eastern and western legs. It continues all the way up to the point when Jesus returns, but having gone through several changes as well. These changes simply make it worse.

While the kingdom retains its iron will, it attempts to "combine with [the clay portion] in the seed of men," but in the end, "they will not adhere to one another" because iron cannot combine with clay or pottery. The concept of combining with the seed of men has been thought to mean many things. Obviously, it can't mean many things and can only mean one thing.

The trouble is trying to understand it as God means it. That's the question ultimately. Some believe it has to do with demons attempting to physically unite with human beings as they may have done in Genesis 6. Others believe that what is being referenced here is the fact that the kingdom will incorporate all people of the world and be-

---

[36] http://www.soniclight.com/constable/notes/pdf/daniel.pdf (3/25/2014)

cause of that cannot mix since Islam retains such a militant dominance. Ultimately, each person will have to decide for himself what he believes the phrase means.

Dr. Thomas Constable has an interesting view on the make-up of the fourth empire in its final stages. It is worth noting.

> *The iron is quite clearly the well-organized imperial rule that allowed Rome to dominate her world. The clay may refer to some form of government that gives more rule to the people, perhaps democracy and or socialism. Perhaps the clay represents the democratic Roman Republic and the iron the imperial Roman Empire. While democratic government has many obvious advantages over other forms of government, particularly the freedoms that its citizens enjoy, it is essentially weak. Its rulers must operate under many checks and balances imposed by the people whom they serve.*[37]

This is an important observation because he then goes onto point out that democracy has its weaknesses. Those weaknesses stem from the fact that citizens exercise freedoms based on specific rights afforded them under the founding documents of that particular society.

Constable speaks of one of the problems of democracy being self-interest. This can be on the part of the citizen or the elected official. In either case, what is often accomplished is not for the benefit of everyone, but for the benefit of groups or factions.

He then goes on to state, "*Another indication that democracy, or socialism, may be what is in view in the clay figure, is that people are essentially clay physically (Gen. 2:7). Rule by the people (i.e., democracy) is rule by clay. Thus it should be no surprise that many students of this*

---

[37] http://www.soniclight.com/constable/notes/pdf/daniel.pdf (3/25/2014)

passage have seen some combination of imperial rule and democracy in the final stage of the fourth (Roman) empire."[38]

This would advance the possibility that in the final stages of the Revised Roman Empire, there is some type of democracy or socialism that boldly contrasts with the imperial rule represented by Islam. We've all seen the bumper sticker that says "Co-Exist" using symbols from several religions to spell out the word.

The problem with it is that Islam (represented by the crescent moon and star, far left) cannot co-exist with any other religion or opposing ideology. Certainly, some would say the same of Christianity, but there is a huge difference.

Christians today are not deliberately burning down mosques or killing Muslims. Yet, this is something that many Muslims do because they believe they must. In doing so, more of the world is "captured" for Allah. This will then usher in the final phase of Allah's kingdom and the Final Mahdi can rise and rule.

Clearly, the final stage of the Roman Empire is one that is iron mixed with clay, though these two materials do not end up mixing at all because it is not possible. The final stage of this empire means that it will be divided until the end. That end comes when Jesus physically returns.

Daniel 2:44-45 highlights the fact of Jesus' return and His Kingdom. As Christians, this is how everything culminates for us. We look for that event, but in the meantime, we continue working. Working, as far as Jesus is concerned, is spreading the Gospel of truth to those who are lost.

> *In the days of those kings the God of heaven will set up a kingdom which will never be destroyed, and that kingdom*

---

[38] http://www.soniclight.com/constable/notes/pdf/daniel.pdf (3/25/2014)

will not be left for another people; it will crush and put an end to all these kingdoms, but it will itself endure forever. Inasmuch as you saw that a stone was cut out of the mountain without hands and that it crushed the iron, the bronze, the clay, the silver and the gold, the great God has made known to the king what will take place in the future; so the dream is true and its interpretation is trustworthy.

It seems very straightforward. God will physically rule and will destroy every man-made kingdom. Only God in Christ will rule and His rule will be the definitive rule, a rule of justice and love, accomplished with a rod of iron.

Chapter 10
Daniel 7

Daniel 2 was certainly interesting because of what it revealed to us. Daniel 7 somewhat reiterates what we learned in Daniel 2 but also adds more detail, going beyond the basics of the type of materials used in the statue and the order in which the empires represented by those materials are presented. In fact, Daniel 7, while actually highlighting the same information given in Daniel 2, does not use the statue from Daniel 2 as its main focal point. Let's take a look!

> *In the first year of Belshazzar king of Babylon Daniel saw a dream and visions in his mind as he lay on his bed; then*

> *he wrote the dream down and related the following summary of it. Daniel said, "I was looking in my vision by night, and behold, the four winds of heaven were stirring up the great sea. And four great beasts were coming up from the sea, different from one another."* (Daniel 7:1-3)

I want to deliberately take small chunks of Scripture here to flesh out the details and not get overwhelmed by the full picture just yet. The above three verses highlight for us when Daniel received this vision. Notice it was not during the reign of Nebuchadnezzar, but of Belshazzar, Nebuchadnezzar's grandson. The time period is 553 BC.

According to Constable, this revelation in Daniel 7 comes 50 years after the first revelation of Daniel 2. Also interesting to note is that Belshazzar was the final king of Babylon, as the kingdom was conquered during his reign by Darius, the Mede. This began the rise of the Medo-Persian Empire.

Notice that in Daniel's dream and visions, he saw that the "great sea" was being stirred up by the four winds. Normally, use of the phrase "great sea" is a reference to the people of the world. Most of us have used or heard the phrase "it was like a sea of people" in describing something in which multitudes of people were present for as far as the eye could see. It's the same concept here for Daniel.

Daniel was either asleep on his bed at night or falling asleep and he saw a dream or visions that gave him a point of view from God's perspective. As God sees the entire world and all its people at the same time, Daniel saw what God sees.

As he continued looking, Daniel saw the "sea" of people being stirred up. Eventually, four great beasts arose from the sea of people and these beasts were different from one another.

What Daniel is describing here is done in different terms than he described in Daniel 2, yet it is the same thing, though from God's perspective. The statue that Nebuchadnezzar saw in Daniel 2 consisted of various sections of different metals, each metal representing a different kingdom.

Here in Daniel 7, we see four separate beasts arising out of the masses of people. We will see that these beasts each represent one particular empire, much the way the specific metals in Daniel 2 represented a unique kingdom.

Constable notes the difference between Daniel 2 and 7 by way of highlighting the outer from the inner aspects of these kingdoms. *"In chapter 2, the four earthly kingdoms and Christ's heavenly kingdom were seen in their outward political appearance; by contrast, chapter 7 presents God's estimate of their innermost moral and spiritual features."*[39]

This is something to keep in mind as we go over the details of each chapter. Daniel 2 presents us with outward manifestations of the empires using an inanimate object (statue) to do so. Aside from the value and strength of the material, we know virtually nothing of the character and/or moral fiber of the kingdom or ruler.

Here in Daniel 7, God is showing Daniel (and us) the moral and spiritual natures of each kingdom, and He does so by using animate objects or beasts. Again, the significance of this should not be lost.

> *The first was like a lion and had the wings of an eagle. I kept looking until its wings were plucked, and it was lifted up from the ground and made to stand on two feet like a man; a human mind also was given to it.*

The above verse – Daniel 7:4 – highlights the first empire, which corresponds with the first empire of Daniel 2, namely, the kingdom of Babylon. Headed by Nebuchadnezzar, it is the most valuable of the

---

[39] http://www.soniclight.com/constable/notes/pdf/daniel.pdf (3/25/2014)

kingdoms but does not have as much strength as the fourth empire, the Roman Empire. Nonetheless, we learn a few more interesting bits of information in verse four.

Notice the first beast is like a lion, but it also has the wings of an eagle. Many nations have used animals to represent themselves. It is no different for Ancient Babylon as well. Images and ancient drawings include lions with wings.

However, the interesting part here is not that the lion with eagle's wings is referenced, but what happens to the lion. The verse specifically states that its wings were plucked and it was made to stand like a man, on two feet.

In Daniel 4, we learn that God did not appreciate Nebuchadnezzar's lack of humility. Because of Nebuchadnezzar's pride and stubborn attitude, God chose to humble him. He did so by removing the king's sovereignty for a time and causing him to live like an animal for a period of seven years (cf. Daniel 4:28-33).

At the end of that time, God restored Nebuchadnezzar to sanity and gave him back his sovereignty over his kingdom. The part of the verse that states "and a human mind was given to him" could easily refer to the return of his sanity (v. 36) after living like an animal for seven years. In the end, and because of this, Nebuchadnezzar realized who was actually in charge of the earth and the universe. The humbling worked and Nebuchadnezzar praised the God of Daniel.

> *But at the end of that period, I, Nebuchadnezzar, raised my eyes toward heaven and my reason returned to me, and I blessed the Most High and praised and honored Him who lives forever;*
>
> *For His dominion is an everlasting dominion, and His kingdom endures from generation to generation. All the inhabitants of the earth are accounted as nothing, but He*

does according to His will in the host of heaven and among the inhabitants of earth; and no one can ward off His hand or say to Him, "What have You done?" (Daniel 4:34-35)

This is what happens when God takes hold of a person and puts him through situations that change him for the better. Nebuchadnezzar was a man whom God purposefully put in place to rule over as much of the earth as he wished. Yet the near-fatal flaw was that he thought he did it by his own power (Daniel 4:30).

God took the king and changed his attitude so that he understood that what he did, he did by God's grace and power. With that lesson learned, God reestablished Nebuchadnezzar as ruler over Babylon.

This is the first "beast," which represents the kingdom of Babylon and Nebuchadnezzar. It is represented from God's perspective as a lion.

The next beast is represented by a bear that is given the command to devour. Daniel 7:5 reveals the details:

And behold, another beast, a second one, resembling a bear. And it was raised up on one side, and three ribs were in its mouth between its teeth; and thus they said to it, "Arise, devour much meat!"

The bear is second to the lion in strength and ferocity. The bear stands leaning or favoring one side, which is likely indicative of the fact that the Medes and Persians were not equal in strength and power. The Persians were the stronger part of the empire.

While possible, it is difficult to know for certain if the three ribs reference nations that the bear devoured, and if so, which nations the three ribs refer to here. "*Some scholars believe the ribs refer to the Babylonian, Lydian, and Egyptian Empires, all of which Medo-Persia conquered eventually. Others suggest that they may refer to Media, Persia, and Babylon, the three major components of the Medo-Persian Empire."*[40]

Nonetheless, the fact that the bear is told to devour much most probably means with respect to the nations and area the bear would conquer in the form of the Medo-Persian Empire.

Daniel 7:6 informs us about the next beast. Again, we should note the difference between this beast (empire) and the previous one.

> *After this I kept looking, and behold, another one, like a leopard, which had on its back four wings of a bird; the beast also had four heads, and dominion was given to it.*

This particular beast, representing the Grecian Empire, led by Alexander the Great, is a leopard with four wings. The wings would certainly signify speed, and when we consider just how quickly Alexander was able to extend the borders of the kingdom that his father before him ruled, the picture is an apt one. Leopards, of course, are fast by themselves, but a leopard with wings would be far faster.

This beast also is said to have four heads. In Daniel 2, the third empire there – also representing the same Grecian Empire – was presented as a metal, bronze. There were no other noticeable factors highlighted in that chapter. Again, though, the purpose of Daniel 2 was to point out the political and outward qualities of each empire. Daniel 7 highlights these same empires, but from God's perspective, which is why we see things in greater detail.

But why four heads? Well, simply put, as we've alluded to in previous chapters, with the sudden and unexpected death of Alexander the Great at the age of 32, his kingdom was essentially left to no one. He did not have a legitimate son/heir at the time of his death (though

---

[40] Ibid., p. 84 (3/25/2014)

Third Beast with Four Heads of Daniel 7

Under Alexander, the Grecian Empire was a cohesive unit. It was only after his death that the empire was subdivided into four parts. This empire is initially represented as one beast that develops four heads.

After Alexander's untimely death, the empire was taken over by four of his generals, each ruling over a fourth of the empire while still maintaining it as the Grecian Empire. These are the four "heads" of Daniel 7.

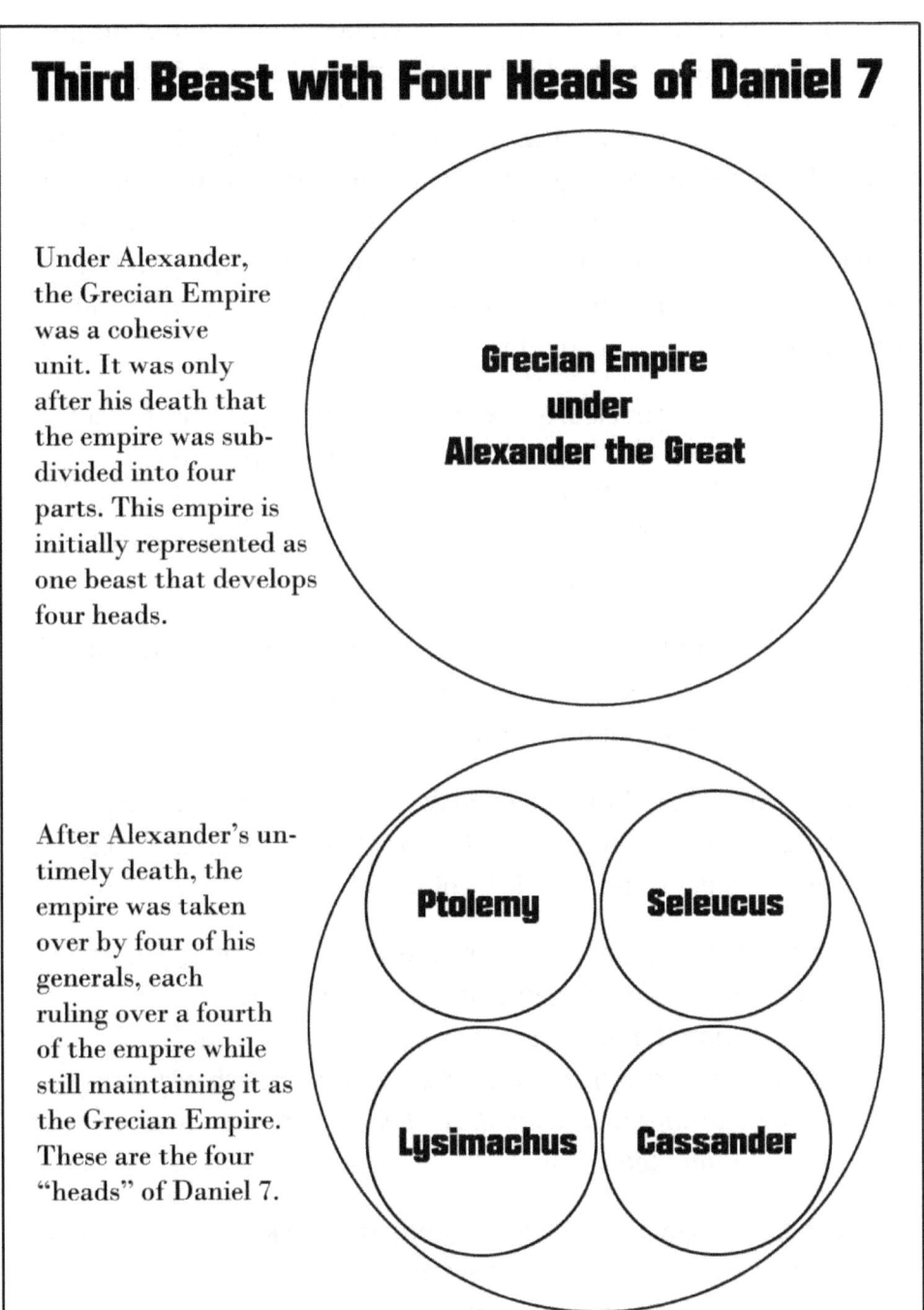

one came several months later from his mistress). Since no heirs existed, the kingdom of Greece was subdivided among four of his generals. Please refer to pages 15, 16, 109, and 123 for reference.

We must remember, when this information was originally given to Daniel the Babylonian Kingdom was still in existence, though during Belshazzar's reign, Darius the Mede conquered the city of Babylon. While Daniel was allowed to see beyond the Babylonian (and the Medo-Persian) empire, he did not personally live to see Alexander become ruler of the Grecian Empire.

In spite of this, we can clearly see that God's Word is very specific. Daniel saw the Grecian Empire at its height and after Alexander's death, when it was subdivided into four sections. These four sections remained as the Grecian Empire but were simply managed by one military general for each section.

This is why the Bible mentions four heads here. Heads in Scripture, unless otherwise noted, always reference a seat of power or rule, much the same way that horns do.

The next two verses of Daniel 7 speak of the next beast and add something to the description that had not been given before. Let's take one verse at a time. Here is Daniel 7:7:

> *After this I kept looking in the night visions, and behold, a fourth beast, dreadful and terrifying and extremely strong; and it had large iron teeth. It devoured and crushed and trampled down the remainder with its feet; and it was different from all the beasts that were before it, and it had ten horns.*

I appreciate the way Daniel keeps saying that he kept looking in the night visions. As intimidating as they may have been, he continued watching them to see what he could learn. His attention to detail has provided us with a good picture of what he saw and ultimately what it all means. Here in this verse, Daniel sees a fourth beast. This fourth beast is the same beast from the statue in Daniel 2 that is made of iron. However, the description here is a bit different because again, we are seeing this now from God's perspective.

This fourth beast is "dreadful and terrifying and extremely strong." That would certainly describe the Roman Empire, as it prompted men to fear the thought of having to fight Roman soldiers.

This beast has "large iron teeth," which makes the connection back to Nebuchadnezzar's statue. Rome there was represented by the iron legs and the feet mixed with iron and clay.

It is reasonable to assume that this picture of the Roman Empire is more toward the time when it was at its height, not at the period when things were in decline. It was so powerful and mighty that not only did it devour other nations and geographic locations, but it literally stamped out everything in its path as it absorbed one nation or group after another. At the height of its power, nothing could stop Rome's march. Nothing.

Notice that this beast is different from all previous beasts, and then we are told that it also had ten horns. Again, horns are symbols of power and rule as used in Scripture. These ten horns coincide with the ten toes. However, there is more information here. In Daniel 2, we simply saw the toes as part of the feet. They were not necessarily imbued with power to rule.

Here in Daniel 7, the same area of the feet is now seen as ten horns. Horns are symbolic of individuals who rule and the same is true here. These ten horns are introduced to us so that we will note that these are more than simply "toes" on a foot. They are leaders, rulers who will have their time to reign. That's all we know about them at this point. We do not know for how long they will rule or what the nature of their rule will be.

If we take it to the logical end, though, it appears as though at some point prior to, but leading up to, the time of the return of Jesus to physically rule over this entire globe, these ten horns (kings) will take their prescribed place on ten thrones for however long God has decreed.

We know it's toward the end of the time that the Revised Roman Empire exists because these ten horns are represented by ten toes in Daniel 2. They're not "knees" that might indicate they rise somewhere in the middle of the Roman Empire. They are toes, and that means that it is toward the very end of the reign after the Roman Empire rises again from what appears to have been a "fatal" wound of history.

Another fascinating piece of information comes our way in the very next verse. Daniel 7:8 provides the information.

> *While I was contemplating the horns, behold, another horn, a little one, came up among them, and three of the first horns were pulled out by the roots before it; and behold, this horn possessed eyes like the eyes of a man and a mouth uttering great boasts.*

What we learn here is that while Daniel is watching this "movie," he has just seen this terrifying fourth beast come along that devours and smashes anything in its path. Daniel sees this beast as something completely different from the other empires. He also sees ten horns, which was something new, as we've explained.

But then, as he continues watching and thinking about what he has just seen regarding the horns, all of a sudden another horn that he describes as "a little one" comes up among the ten. Picture the fact that he has just seen ten horns. He is thinking about what they could possibly mean when he now sees another smaller horn rise up out of or among the original ten. As he continues to look, three of the origin-

Fourth Beast with Ten Horns of Daniel 7

Phase 1

Original ten horns are associated with the fourth beast. These are the ten toes of Daniel 2.

Phase 2

Out of the original ten horns, another "smaller" horn rises up to take his place among them. This smaller horn becomes the **ELEVENTH**.

Phase 3

After the smaller ELEVENTH horn rises, three of the original ten horns are "uprooted" (killed/die). The smaller horn is now the **EIGHTH**.

nal ten horns are literally uprooted. This is a poetic way of saying that the three rulers were killed or died in some fashion.

We had ten horns. Another smaller one rises out of but was not one of the original ten. Now we have *eleven* horns total. But then, three horns are killed or die. That leaves seven of the original horns and the one smaller horn, for a total of *eight*. It is important to make a mental note of this because this motif will come up again when we get into Revelation 13 and 17.

What we need to figure out, of course, is not only who the leaders are who are represented by the original ten horns, but who the smaller horn is as well. Before we do that, we want to take a look at Revelation 13 and 17 to see if God provides us any more detail concerning these beasts.

Before we get there, let's look again at Daniel 7. Is there anything else we can discern from this chapter that will help us understand the situation?

Verse eight continues by telling us that the "*horn possessed eyes like the eyes of a man and a mouth uttering great boasts.*" He appears every bit human here, with eyes like those of a man, and he obviously has a brain that allows him to boast great things. The boasts are about himself and what he hopes to accomplish. This will be fleshed out a bit more in Revelation.

However, if we look at what the apostle Paul says in 2 Thessalonians 2:3b-12, we learn a bit more about this man. Let's take a moment or two to look at these verses in Thessalonians to see what Paul says about this same man referred to in Daniel 7:8.

> *3b...and the man of lawlessness is revealed, the son of destruction, 4 who opposes and exalts himself above every so-called god or object of worship, so that he takes his seat in the temple of God, displaying himself as being God.*

5 Do you not remember that while I was still with you, I was telling you these things? 6 And you know what restrains him now, so that in his time he will be revealed. 7 For the mystery of lawlessness is already at work; only he who now restrains will do so until he is taken out of the way. 8 Then that lawless one will be revealed whom the Lord will slay with the breath of His mouth and bring to an end by the appearance of His coming; 9 that is, the one whose coming is in accord with the activity of Satan, with all power and signs and false wonders, 10 and with all the deception of wickedness for those who perish, because they did not receive the love of the truth so as to be saved. 11 For this reason God will send upon them a deluding influence so that they will believe what is false, 12 in order that they all may be judged who did not believe the truth, but took pleasure in wickedness.

Taking note of the verse numbers left in for ease of reference, notice that Paul is responding to a question posed to him by the people at Thessalonica (via Timothy). He tells them that the "day of the Lord" cannot happen until the man of lawlessness is revealed. The man of lawlessness is the way Paul refers to the coming Antichrist. Paul then goes on to note a few things about the Antichrist that tell us more about his character and what type of person he is going to be.

Notice that in verse four, Paul tells us that this man of lawlessness will take his place in a seat in the Holy Place (the rebuilt Jewish Temple). Once there, he will declare himself to actually be God. This will be the biggest boast that the Antichrist can come up with, that he is God. He will then demand that people worship him because of this claim and many will unfortunately do just that.

The remainder of the verses quoted point out how this man of lawlessness, or Antichrist, will come to his end. It will happen as the

Lord Jesus physically returns to this earth at the very end of the Tribulation/Great Tribulation. That will signal the end of this age.

However, let's not forget verses nine and ten because they tell us that this Antichrist will rise to power on earth because he is completely sold out to Satan and his schemes. The sin that caused Satan to fall was pride in thinking that he was equal to God (Isaiah 14; Ezekiel 28). This egoism or narcissistic attitude overcame Satan (Lucifer before his fall), driving him to contemplate that God wasn't so great and that he (Satan) could be like him. The idea that a created being could not only think like this but come to believe it seems absurd, yet most of us know what truly narcissistic people can be like. They are so drawn to themselves that they see little else. Their minds are clouded with lies about their own alleged greatness. They are often very intelligent, if not brilliant, people, and they tend to attract people to themselves.

People like this often tend to think they can do anything, and more often than not they become psychopaths, using people to obtain what they want but having no real feeling or compassion for anyone. They make the best con artists in the world because they are able to understand what people need to feel good about themselves.

I believe that this is why Paul tells us that Satan comes to deceive us and is able to do so because of his ability to transform himself into an angel of light (cf. 2 Corinthians 11:14). A person who loves himself so much is usually a master manipulator, getting people to do his bidding because it serves his purposes. Most are blind to this and fail to understand what's going on beneath the surface.

This is why people like Ted Bundy can last for years without getting caught, and when they are caught, people have such a difficult time accepting the fact that these killers are essentially psychopaths who have absolutely no feeling for anyone else. They are at the center of their world and they make everyone their servants without them even realizing it.

This is Satan times one thousand. He will imbue his spiritual son – Antichrist – with all of his power and even his throne in order to attempt to achieve what he has always desired: to be like the Most High. He will go to the man who turns out to be the Antichrist and offer him the same thing he offered Jesus as recorded in Matthew 4 when Jesus was led by the Spirit into the wilderness to be tempted by the devil.

There, Satan tempted Jesus to worship him as God and in return he would give him all the kingdoms of the world. Jesus responded with a firm "no," but the Antichrist will not. He will gladly agree to the exchange because it will give him what he desires more than anything. It will provide him with the power to do miracles and be worshipped.

In essence, Satan himself will be the one who is being worshipped, and in that sense, he will see part of his promise to become like the Most High achieved on a human level. But like everything that Satan does, it will not be the same thing and it will pale in comparison to actually being God, something Satan will never achieve because at best, he is the most brilliant of all created beings, but created nonetheless.

Satan will take this "smaller" horn, who at first is the eleventh, but after three of the ten horns mysteriously die will become the eighth, and use this smaller horn to make himself great. Satan will have seven years to make it happen, but in the end, Paul tells us (as does Daniel) that Jesus will return and take charge by killing the Antichrist with a word (or breath) from His mouth.

Chapter 11
Revelation 13, Part 1

Revelation 13 starts with the action already happening. John says that he sees the dragon (Satan) standing on the shore near the sea and a beast is rising out of the sea. We already know that the use of the word "sea" here simply means the mass of people throughout the world. Let's look at the first six verses.

> 1 And the dragon stood on the sand of the seashore. Then I saw a beast coming up out of the sea, having ten horns and seven heads, and on his horns were ten diadems, and on his heads were blasphemous names. 2 And the beast

> *which I saw was like a leopard, and his feet were like those of a bear, and his mouth like the mouth of a lion. And the dragon gave him his power and his throne and great authority. 3 I saw one of his heads as if it had been slain, and his fatal wound was healed. And the whole earth was amazed and followed after the beast; 4 they worshiped the dragon because he gave his authority to the beast; and they worshiped the beast, saying, "Who is like the beast, and who is able to wage war with him?" 5 There was given to him a mouth speaking arrogant words and blasphemies, and authority to act for forty-two months was given to him. 6 And he opened his mouth in blasphemies against God, to blaspheme His name and His tabernacle, that is, those who dwell in heaven.*

There is quite a bit happening here, but by now, much of it should strike familiar chords within you because of what we have already gone over. As we know, the dragon is standing on the seashore, and he and John are seeing the same scene unfold. A beast rises out of the sea.

The beast now has seven heads and ten horns. Beyond this, the beast's horns wear ten diadems, or crowns. Let's discuss this before moving on.

Recall from the last chapter that we learned that one of the beasts referenced in Daniel 7 had four heads. We learned that this was a reference to the Grecian Empire after Alexander had died and four of his generals took it over, with each taking a fourth of the kingdom to control. It was still the Grecian Empire, though.

Then why does this chapter in Revelation talk about a beast having *seven* heads? Simply put, this beast that comes up out of the sea at this point is a conglomeration of all the empires that came before the fourth empire. The only "empire" missing from the picture, because it is not part of this beast, is the Messianic Kingdom, which will be instituted when the Lord returns physically. It is important to understand that the Bible teaches that Jesus will return physically, though a popular belief today is that He will return spiritually, and in fact many say He has done so.

The problem with this view is that it really is not supported by Scripture if Scripture is allowed to interpret itself and if the Bible is understood in its most plain, ordinary sense.

For instance, one of the best proofs that Jesus will return physically is found in His own words in Matthew 24. Here, in the Olivet Discourse, Jesus points out many of the things that will take place leading up to the time of His return. Then, He actually speaks about His physical return in Matthew 24:29-31.

> *But immediately after the tribulation of those days the sun will be darkened, and the moon will not give its light, and the stars will fall from the sky, and the powers of the heavens will be shaken. And then the sign of the Son of Man will appear in the sky, and then all the tribes of the earth will mourn, and they will see the Son of Man coming on the clouds of the sky with power and great glory. And He will send forth His angels with a great trumpet and they will gather together His elect from the four winds, from one end of the sky to the other.*

Notice that after the Tribulation, the sign of the Son of Man will appear. What is that sign? The actual physical return of Jesus Himself is highlighted here. His return will herald a new age and His second coming will be seen by everyone (all the tribes of the earth will mourn).

Jesus speaks of the fact that He will be returning to this earth after the Tribulation of the coming last days. Some erroneously believe this refers to the AD 70 event when Roman armies surrounded and destroyed Jerusalem and the Jewish Temple. Yes, that was certainly God's judgment on the nation of Israel for rejecting Jesus, the Messiah. However, He did not return in any sense at that time, though people believe He returned spiritually. There is no such thing in the Bible.

For further proof, we need only turn to Acts 1. Here, Jesus gives His followers final instructions. Then He is taken up to heaven and hidden in the clouds. While the men are still standing there looking up in the sky, two other "men" (angels) come along and ask them why they are looking up in the sky. The exact words were (Acts 1:11):

> *Men of Galilee, why do you stand looking into the sky?*
> *This Jesus, who has been taken up from you into heaven,*
> *will come in just the same way as you have watched Him*
> *go into heaven.*

It's an interesting question. But notice they answer it before the disciples get a chance. The angels tell the men that this very same Jesus – who was taken up into heaven – will return exactly the way He left.

There is no other way to interpret this than taking it to mean that Jesus will return physically. This verse, coupled with Jesus' own words about His own return (not to mention numerous passages in the Old Testament as well as the New), point out that His return will be seen by every eye on earth. It will not be an invisible, spiritual return.

Once Jesus returns, He will immediately begin preparations to set up His own Kingdom. That kingdom will completely erase and replace all previous human kingdoms.

The beast that John sees coming out of the sea (of nations) represents all the previous empires that have come, starting with Nebuchadnezzar's kingdom of Babylon. Let's take a closer look so we fully understand where the seven "heads" come from and how they are determined. We certainly need to understand this aspect of things, because if we don't, we will wrongly interpret this or other areas of Scripture.

As can be seen from the illustration (page 123), the original four beasts of Daniel 2 each had one head. Together, there were four beasts, which represented four empires, and if each had one head, then that would total four heads. We also have the illustration on page 109 that highlights specifically the third beast (Greece) and shows how it became a beast with four heads.

But also note that after Alexander's death at the age of 32, since he had no legitimate heir, his empire was divided (though it remained the Grecian Empire in its entirety) among his generals. What was once a beast with one head now became a beast with four separate heads. Daniel 7 references these as four "horns" in verse six, but all the horns are applied to the same beast.

The original four heads (one for each beast) then became a total of seven heads (when we consider each general having one head). Babylon had one head, Medo-Persian had one head (because each ruler ruled separately), the Grecian empire now had four heads, and the Roman Empire had one head. This provided a grand total of seven heads that we see in Revelation 13.

We also need to remember that when Daniel saw these beasts, he lived during the time of Babylon and into the Medo-Persian empires. Much of Nebuchadnezzar's statue is yet before him in the future.

By the time the apostle John wrote Revelation, much of Nebuchadnezzar's statue from Daniel 2 was behind him. In fact, as he lived, the Roman Empire (the fourth beast) was in existence. It had not yet split into an eastern and western leg and certainly had not reached the point where there were ten toes of clay and iron. Nonetheless, John could look back in history and know that Babylon had existed then

The Seven-Headed Beast of Revelation 13

The **FOUR** beasts of Daniel 2 consist of the empires noted above.

Then, Alexander died and empire was divied among generals.

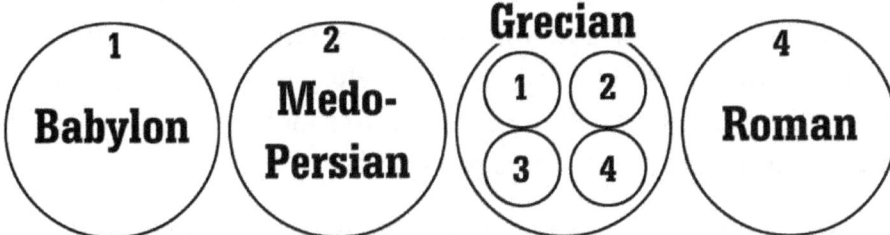

The Grecian beast went through a change. It went from having just one head (Alexander) to having four heads (after his death). At that point, the beasts had a total of 7 heads. Babylon, Medo-Persia, and Roman consist of one head each (3 total) but now the Grecian has four heads (3 + 4 = 7).

came the Medo-Persian Empire. This was followed by Alexander's Grecian Empire, including the time after it had been divided into sub-kingdoms, yet remained part of the original Grecian Empire. John saw all of that. There was only some of the Roman Empire left before him as it would segue into what would become its final stages.

The fact that this particular beast with seven heads has parts of each beast is telling. It points out that though each new empire came along and replaced the previous one, it absorbed aspects of that previous empire. Here is Revelation 13:2 again.

> *And the beast which I saw was like a leopard, and his feet were like those of a bear, and his mouth like the mouth of a lion. And the dragon gave him his power and his throne and great authority.*

Note the beast is like a leopard (Greece overall), but his feet were like a bear (Medo-Persian) and his mouth like a lion (Babylon). The leopard represented the Grecian Empire, the bear represented the Medo-Persian Empire, and the lion represented the Babylonian Empire.

This final beast is truly a conglomeration of all previous empires going back to Nebuchadnezzar's Babylon. This is likely one of the reasons John found it so frightening. Imagine seeing the image of it. Also remember, these are character traits of what the beast's character will be like. It is not simply the beast's outer look. They represent the moral or spiritual nature of this beast.

Note also that the dragon gives this beast (at this stage) his own power, his own throne, and great authority. Certainly, that authority and power is limited by God Himself; nonetheless, Satan (the dragon) is still the ruler of the powers of the air (Ephesians 2:2). He has tremendous authority and ability that God has allowed him to keep even though he is a completely defeated foe.

Does it sound like Satan is putting all of his apples in one basket here? It's because he is doing just that. He is banking on winning the war with God via this beast in its final stages. He literally imbues the fourth beast – whose ruler is Antichrist – with his own power and authority. That tells us that Satan has no plan B and is counting on the Antichrist to win the battle as he works through him to thwart God's plans. Anyone who mistakenly believes that Satan has been declawed is in for a shock. As Christians, we are on God's side. He empowers us and greater is He that is in us than he that is in the world (1 John 4:4).

Nonetheless, it is extremely important that we do not stupidly misunderstand Satan's power. He does not answer to us. He answers to the Lord. He is not afraid of us. He is only afraid of the Lord. Is it any wonder why Michael, the archangel, did not take Satan on directly, but simply said, "The Lord rebuke you!" when Satan was trying to steal the body of Moses in Jude 1:9?

We need to respect the fact that God allows Satan to continue to possess and exercise great power among those who follow him. We cannot afford to be irresponsible here.

This tremendous power will at some point in the future become part of the man of lawlessness. He will be Satan's arm in this realm. He and Satan will be of one mind and Antichrist will endeavor to do all that Satan wishes. Antichrist will be a man so possessed of Satan that where he ends and Satan begins will not be definable.

The next verse, Revelation 13:3, points out that one of the heads is fatally wounded: *"I saw one of his heads as if it had been slain, and his fatal wound was healed. And the whole earth was amazed and followed after the beast."*

This verse is most often associated with the Antichrist. Commentators say that this is the way Antichrist attempts to portray Jesus in that he dies and then comes back to life as though mirroring the death and resurrection of Jesus. I used to think that as well, but the reality is that John is speaking of the beast with seven heads here. Antichrist will not have seven heads. He will look every bit a man, completely in human form, because he will be a man, supernaturally endowed with diabolical power from Satan.

Since the context is about the beast with seven heads (representing the previous empires) then it is very likely that one of the heads re

Rome Rising

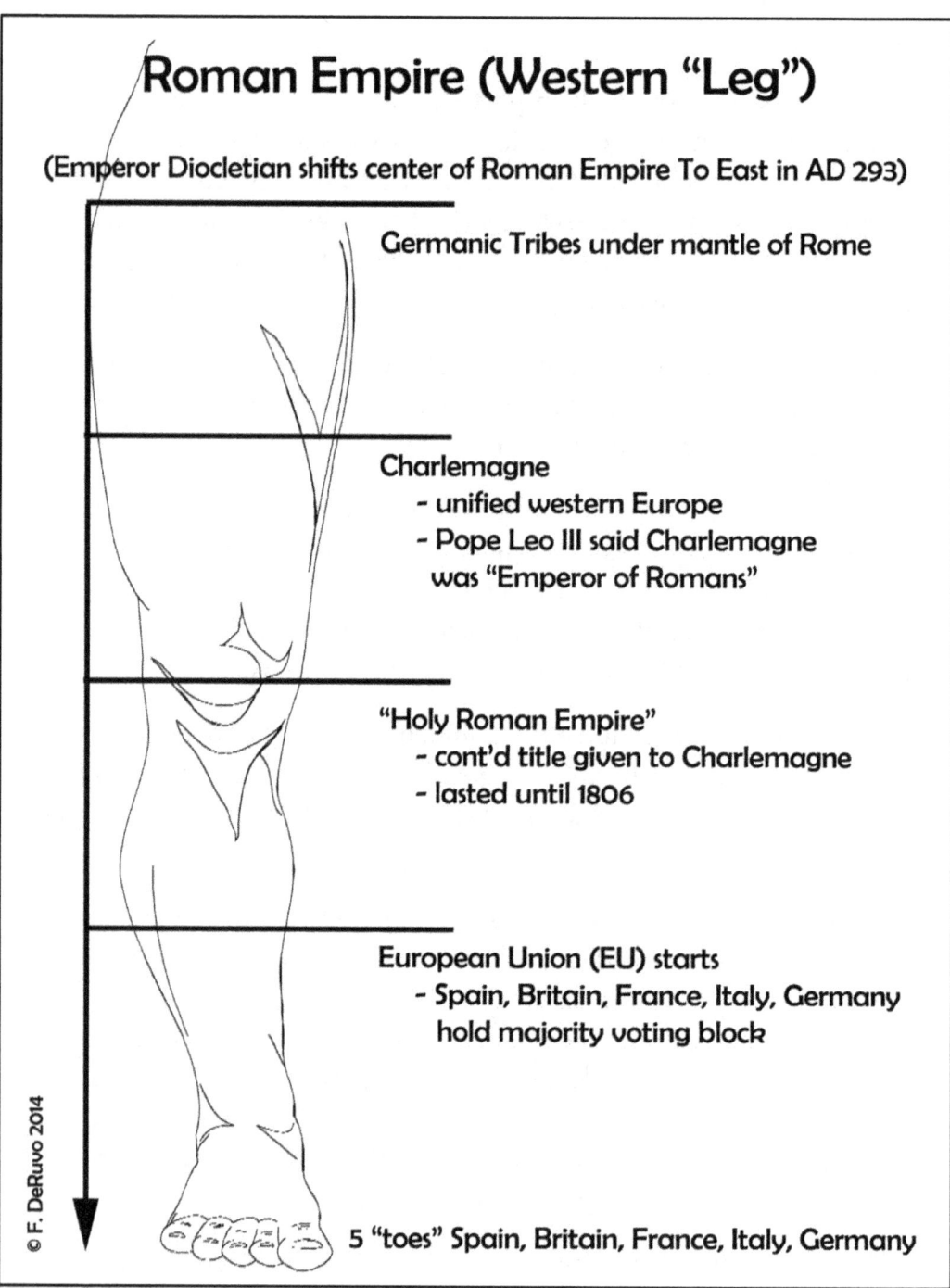

Rome Rising

Roman Empire (Eastern "Leg")

(Emperor Diocletian shifts center of Roman Empire To East in AD 293)

Emperor Diocletian and Tetrarchy

Constantine and Byzantine Empire

Turkey & Ottoman Empire (Caliphate)
(included Islamic ideology)

Countries w/Islamic roots
(Toward new Caliphate)

© F. DeRuvo 2014

5 "toes" Turkey, Syira, Egypt, Iran, Iraq?

ferred to has to do with a specific empire, not a man who heads up that empire. I believe that John sees one of the heads of the beast that appears to die.

If this head represents an empire (as we believe it does), then it must be referring to one of the empires that seems to die. Since all empires previous to the Roman Empire appeared to be conquered and taken over by a new ruler who created a new empire, it seems that the only empire that seems to have "died" was the Roman Empire.

We've discussed how the Roman Empire went through various changes, first splitting into two legs, the eastern and western. From there, we noted that each leg had a different ruler.

The western leg was actually ruled by Germanic tribes, and then Charlemagne became the Holy Roman Emperor. Following Charlemagne, the western leg became simply the Holy Roman Empire essentially controlled by the Roman Catholic Church. This ultimately gave way to the European Union, which is what exists today.

The eastern leg was originally controlled by Emperor Diocletian and the Tetrarchy. Diocletian was the individual who actually began to focus on the eastern leg of the Roman Empire. From there, it was Constantine and the Byzantine Empire. This eventually succumbed to the Ottoman Empire and Turkish rule. The final stage of the eastern leg is no real empire at all, but a mass of Islamic countries composed of Muslims doing their best to bring forth the next caliphate (Islamic rule) throughout the world.

We noted that because of Islam's inability to cooperate with other groups, the final stage of the fourth beast – the ten toes – will easily be defined as iron (Islam) mixed with clay (rest of the populace). This tension will last until Jesus returns. As for the countries represented by each toe, it is our best guess that the countries we have listed in each chart are those countries. Certainly it makes sense that the eastern leg's final component will be comprised of countries that are Islamic and exist under some form of Sharia law.

The countries for the western leg of the old Roman Empire could very well be represented by those countries currently in the European Union who maintain the largest voting block out of all 28 countries that are part of the EU. Again, these are best guesses.

The next verse (four) of Revelation 13 is interesting, to say the least, and I believe it's where folks get the idea that verse three speaks of a man, not an empire. It states, *"they worshiped the dragon because he gave his authority to the beast; and they worshiped the beast, saying, 'Who is like the beast, and who is able to wage war with him?'"*

Because this verse immediately follows verse three, it appears as though it points back to the beast and the fact that though it appeared dead, it was now alive again. That could well be, but I also wonder if the people worship it because of the fact that it has accomplished a number of things as it grew to maturity (or came back from the dead)?

For instance, this last beast – what we'll call the Revised Roman Empire – obviously must become dominant in the world. In order to do so, things like Christianity have to be either ignored or punished in some way. The world is rapidly moving toward that.

As this is being written, Hobby Lobby is presenting arguments before the Supreme Court of the United States in the case *Sabellius vs. Hobby Lobby* because they do not believe that they should be forced to provide health insurance that includes prescriptive medication that will forcibly abort unborn babies. Of course, Planned Parenthood is lying that Hobby Lobby does not want to provide birth control medication. This is not true, but to Planned Parenthood, pills that cause abortions are the same as birth control.

Hobby Lobby is owned by Christians. They do not want to be forced to provide things to their employees that go against their religious beliefs. If an employee has an abortion on their own, while the Christian owners of Hobby Lobby would not like it, it wouldn't be something they were part of because the employee made the decision and paid for it (or used federal funds).

Hobby Lobby objects to the federal government saying that the health insurance that they offer to employees (and subsidize) must include medication that causes abortions. This is one way that the federal government is running roughshod over Christians and Christianity. At the same time, this same federal government is opening the door wide for Muslims and Islam. Apparently, there is no issue regarding separation of church and state when it comes to the religion of Islam, but there is an issue when it deals with Christianity.

But it's not simply the federal government that is putting the squeeze on Christians in America. Organizations that have been evangelical in nature since their inception appear to be jumping the shark.

Throughout the world, Satan is rising up against God and those who belong to Him. This should definitely not come as a shock because Jesus warned us, as did Paul, Peter, and other writers of the New Testament.

Whether it has to do with Muslims in Egypt burning down churches (sometimes with Christian worshipers still inside), the federal government wanting to force Christians to align themselves with policies and laws that are opposed to God's law, or non-Christians attempting to put Christians who own businesses out of business, it is clear that the attacks have begun in earnest. Not only will Satan not stop, but he will continue his efforts to box in and defeat Christians as the time draws closer for his final demise.

In essence, the tone of civility is being removed from society and has been for many decades. I believe it has now reached a near-fever pitch and the goal is so close that those in Satan's kingdom of darkness can taste it. They want Christianity stopped, defeated, and erased from society because it is a constant reminder of how far they have fallen.

Moreover, Christianity is something that people have no real answer to, though they certainly believe they do. I don't even truly believe that people understand their anger toward Christianity and Christians (for those who have it). Their reaction is characteristic of Satan's anger because he knows his time is short. The people who reflect that same anger have no real clue as to why they feel as they do.

I believe when things reach critical mass and what is now being held back is released (2 Thessalonians 2:6-7), all hell will literally break loose. The fact that people are worshiping the beast may be due to the fact that the beast is seen as the one who vanquished Christianity. For the lost of this world, that would certainly be something to get excited about.

We know that during the final stages of this fourth beast, the world will be different. It will come under the power of Satan's deception, and interestingly enough, God says that He Himself will cause the delusion to be so strong that people will believe the lie. In fact, it will be so strong that if it were possible, even the elect would be deceived. Fortunately, the implication is that this is not possible (cf. Matthew 24:24; Mark 13:22). I'm not sure we can fully appreciate the power of such a deception, but I do believe we have seen the beginnings of it with the election of President Obama.

Think about how, during his first run for office, people seemed unable to think logically. Their emotion carried them and they ignored things like his absolute and unfailing support for abortion. He was a good speaker, almost hypnotic. He would say things like, "Change is coming!" and while no one knew what that meant specifically, he never bothered to explain it in detail, preferring to allow people to come up with their own ideas about what it meant.

Since President Obama has taken office, we've heard one celebrity after another talk about how great he is, and Jamie Foxx at one point referred to President Obama as "our lord and savior."[41] Most people in the audience clapped at the remark. Chris Rock said that we should do what President Obama wanted because we should see him as though he is our father, the boss of the country.[42]

More recently, Russell Crowe called President Obama the "light and the future."[43] Not only do too many celebrities speak highly of President Obama, but it's rare to hear a negative word coming from the press. It's almost as though it is wrong to speak against President Obama because he is considered sacrosanct. Yet no other president has enjoyed such privilege and has always been fair game.

This is a problem that seems to have only gotten worse during his second term. There is a great deal of protecting going on as if it borders on illegal to speak against President Obama. I believe this has to do with those who are trying hard to protect him because they still have a good deal of work for him to do before the end of his second term. I also believe it is the start of the delusion that is overtaking this country and eventually the world.

It's a delusion that refuses to die and seems to be getting stronger. When President Obama does things that are seen as illegal (bypassing the Constitution, for instance), Congress doesn't know how to respond. They then try to pass a law that is designed to force President

---

[41] http://www.huffingtonpost.com/2012/11/27/jamie-foxx-obama-lord-and-savior-furor-soul-train-awards_n_2199439.html (3/26/2014)
[42] http://www.washingtontimes.com/blog/inside-politics/2013/feb/6/chris-rock-president-obama-our-boss-dad-country/ (3/26/2014)
[43] http://twitchy.com/2012/10/21/russell-crowe-says-obama-is-the-light-and-the-future-then-throws-hissy-fit-blocks-fans/ (3/26/2014)

Obama to observe and obey law, created by Rep. Trey Gowdy (R-SC).[44]

If members of Congress feel the need to create a law that is designed to force President Obama to obey the law, then it's clear that they believe he is outside the law. This makes him a lawless president, something that the coming Antichrist will most certainly be (man of lawlessness). I'm not saying that President Obama is the Antichrist. I'm simply saying that many of the things he does or attempts to do are outside the law.

But our entire society has been force-fed lawlessness and anti-Christian ranting for so long that it was bound to become part of the way society thinks. This is what has now become commonplace in society throughout the world. It's as though we are living during the time of Nero when the world wanted to place the blame somewhere and Christians are supposed to turn the other cheek, so why not them?

If we look long and hard at Paul's description of what society will be like toward the end of this age (as referenced in 2 Timothy 3), it is not difficult to look around and see that these attitudes are already here to a degree. They will simply worsen as time marches onward.

When we couple this attitude with the delusion that is permeating society as a whole, then we begin to see a picture of what things will be like when the final stages of the fourth beast take solid shape. Eventually, the ten toes, which are also the ten kings, will rise to take their place in history, and when that happens, Antichrist will rise among them.

It will be a perfect time for him to make his move too, because he will know without doubt who the ten kings are and whom he must over-

---

[44] http://gopthedailydose.com/2014/03/12/now-in-house-trey-gowdys-bill-to-force-obama-to-obey-the-laws/ (3/26/2014)

come in order to become number one, the man in charge. But please note, the fourth beast will have already "risen" by the time the ten kings take their place. The world will have become one in purpose, with one system connecting all areas of the world. I believe the ten kings will rise up simply because it makes sense to break the entire globe down into ten parts – each part headed by one person – to make things far more manageable.

When this happens, the Antichrist will rise to the top and will claim the place that Satan has carved out for him. Antichrist will have no problem running the entire world. This has been a rather longish explanation of why the world will be willing to worship the beast (the final stages of the fourth beast, or the Revised Roman Empire) and the Antichrist along with it.

People are so impressed with the final stages of the fourth beast that they even rhetorically ask who can make war with him. This beast is powerful, and the man who ends up controlling it will also be powerful. The question – who can make war with him – is rhetorical because no one really believes war can come against the beast. This is how confident people become due to the delusion that has captured their minds. The next few verses of Revelation 13 provide even more insight.

> *There was given to him a mouth speaking arrogant words and blasphemies, and authority to act for forty-two months was given to him. And he opened his mouth in blasphemies against God, to blaspheme His name and His tabernacle, that is, those who dwell in heaven.*

These verses – five and six – tell us more about the Antichrist, the mouth of the beast. He is, above all things, arrogant. Everything he says is based on this arrogance, and though what he utters is blasphemy, the world is enamored because it's what they think as well. Antichrist – as head of the fourth beast at this future time – is exactly what the world wants. They want someone who will tell them it's okay to reject God because they are gods! He will be the consummate New Age proponent, at least for a time, for the first 42 months, or 3 ½ years.

He wants to disarm everyone, helping them to appreciate their inner deity. Yes, Christians had it wrong all along. There is no one God because we are all gods.

God grants Antichrist the authority to act and speak these blasphemies for three and a half years. Antichrist wastes no time using every opportunity to blaspheme God Almighty, His Name, His tabernacle and heaven itself. He knows that he has three and a half years and nothing will happen to him during that time.

Why wouldn't this type of behavior be attractive to the world? Why wouldn't this type of action and speech be something that the world is dying to have? It encourages them to do the same thing! It forces them to open themselves up to Satan and his minions.

I believe that during the coming Tribulation, the denizens of hell will be let loose from hell itself and given even greater freedom to possess and inflict evil on the world's populace. Remember, Satan gives his power, authority, and throne to the Antichrist. I don't think we can fully comprehend how evil and brutal life will be at this point in time.

Satan, through the Antichrist and the beast empire under his control, will take over all aspects of society, creating hell on earth. The world will go along with it because of their hatred of Christianity and Christians.

As Satan empowers and works through Antichrist, he will infect the world with his evil, and what we think of as evil now will pale in comparison then. Think of a president who would stand at the podium and blaspheme God on a daily basis. If any elected official did that now, too many Christians to count would protest. God works through His Church to hold back the full power of evil, but one day, that restraining influence will be gone. Frankly, I cannot picture unbridled evil running rampant throughout society, can you?

But things will become thoroughly evil. Revelation 13:7 states, *"It was also given to him to make war with the saints and to overcome them, and authority over every tribe and people and tongue and nation was given to him."*

Clearly, Antichrist's authority extends to being able to make war with the saints and to overcome them. This includes Christians of every tribe, people, tongue, and nation. God allows it for His own purposes and we'd best not question why.

This is Satan's time. He will have his way. God gives him every opportunity to make his promises come to fruition, the promises of Isaiah 14 and Ezekiel 28. This is when he said, among other things, that he would become like the Most High.

It's been thousands of years, but the day is almost upon us when Satan will be allowed the sort of freedom that he can use to make his promises a reality. He will have power. God will even help him by sending a delusion, making it easier for Satan to overcome people and cause them to follow him.

God will allow Satan to be the living embodiment of arrogance and to blaspheme in the person of the Antichrist. He will have virtually no limits to what he can do in this realm and he will always have his dutiful army of fallen angels and demons to help him. Much of the world will join with him in his blaspheme, yet not all.

Those who fail to follow him and worship him will be killed, and I'm sure this will be done with glee. The world will also roar with excitement. Who knows, but the execution of Christians may once again become the entertainment of the future. It's very possible and very likely.

Verses eight and nine of Revelation 13 note quite succinctly, *"All who dwell on the earth will worship him, everyone whose name has not been written from the foundation of the world in the book of life of the Lamb who has been slain. If anyone has an ear, let him hear."*

Everyone whose name was not written in the book of life from the very creation of the world will worship the beast. The phrase "if anyone has an ear, let him hear" is a dire warning for anyone who is willing to listen. Are you concerned about your salvation? If so, then it would be very wise of you to ensure that you are saved, that you might spend eternity with Christ in perfection.

Nonetheless, there will be multitudes of people who will worship the beast. They will fall in line and do everything they are supposed to do because they value their own lives above doing what is right. They will not question. They will obey.

The Antichrist will run a tight ship. He will expect people to bow to him and worship him. He will be seen as God or else. Pity the person who does not ask, "How high?" when Antichrist says, "JUMP!"

Chapter 12
Revelation 13, Part 2

The remaining verses of Revelation 13 introduce another beast. This beast is described for us and appears to be something less powerful than the first beast.

11 Then I saw another beast coming up out of the earth; and he had two horns like a lamb and he spoke as a dragon. 12 He exercises all the authority of the first beast in his presence. And he makes the earth and those who dwell in it to worship the first beast, whose fatal wound was healed. 13 He performs great signs, so that he even makes fire come down out of heaven to the earth in the presence of men. 14 And he deceives those who dwell on the earth because of the signs which it was given him to perform in the presence of the beast, telling those who dwell on the earth to make an image to the beast who had the wound of the sword and has come to life. 15 And it was given to him to give breath to the image of the beast, so that the image of the beast would even speak and cause as many as do not worship the image of the beast to be killed. 16 And he causes all, the small and the great, and the rich and the poor, and the free men and the slaves, to be given a mark on their right hand or on their forehead, 17 and he provides that no one will be able to buy or to sell, except the one who has the mark, either the name of the beast or the number of his name. 18 Here is wisdom. Let him who has understanding calculate the number of the beast, for the number is that of a man; and his number is six hundred and sixty-six.

Again, the numerical verse references are left in to make it easier to refer to specific verses. First, we learn that this second beast comes up out of the earth and he has two horns – small horns – like a lamb, but he speaks like a dragon.

How does the dragon speak? He speaks with deceptive, arrogant, and blasphemous verbiage. He speaks out of pride. Though he appears like a lamb – cute, cuddly, non-threatening – he is inwardly a dragon who will devour anyone who stands in his way. In fact, through his constant use of deception, he hopes to devour men spiritually so that they never gain salvation.

This is the persona that takes people by surprise. He is another consummate conman. He presents himself as disarming to people, which causes people to let down their guards. His words, though soothing, are deadly. They rob people of eternal life before they have a chance to understand what eternal life is all about.

Verse 12 tells us that this second beast exercises all authority of the first beast. This is useful to the first beast because there is someone else who will toot the first beast's horn, and it's not the first beast (solely).

This second beast puts all of his effort into pumping up the first beast. He even performs miracles that shine the spotlight on the first beast. He causes fire to come down from heaven, whether real or by use of technology or holograms. Because of this and his association with the first beast, people marvel.

There is a lot happening in these verses. We learn that this second beast is sold out to the first beast. He demands that the people of the earth make a statue of the first beast. He then somehow animates it or makes it appear as if he does.

With the technology that exists today, including what we likely do not even know about (used in military operations), it will probably be very easy for this second beast to animate the first beast. At the same time, because of the realism of holograms that we know of now, it makes one wonder what type of trickery will be used to cause the statue of the first beast to appear to come alive.

Not long ago, a type of hologram was used to make it appear as though rapper Tupac Shakur was alive again. Videos of the event can be found on the Internet by simply searching for his name. However, be warned that if the video is located, the language is not family-friendly. The point is that appearing to make someone alive who is dead is not that difficult to do.

The hologram used to recreate Tupac essentially has three parts to it. First, the performer (in Tupac's case, Snoop Dogg) stands behind an angled transparent foil on stage, out of sight of the audience. Second, the image of the person (Tupac) is projected onto the floor surface in front of the stage. Third, the image bounces back onto the transparent foil and the audience sees the image but not the foil (or the performer).

If that is the case, then my assumption is that whatever the second beast does is going to have to be absolutely astounding, something that people have not seen before. It may well be completely supernatural in nature, having nothing to do with computerized technology. At this point, of course, we simply don't know. But we do know that what we have seen as holograms are not technically true holograms like we see in movie representations.

It is very possible that the same supernatural power that energizes the first beast (empire headed by Antichrist) will also energize the second beast to an extent. The obvious connection is that both of these beasts have components that speak like the dragon. The other obvious connection is that both of these beasts fully oppose the Living God and support Satan in his efforts to overthrow God.

Admittedly, the verbiage of these verses is difficult to interpret. Verse 15 states, *"And it was given to him to give breath to the image of the beast, so that the image of the beast would even speak and cause as many as do not worship the image of the beast to be killed."*

Remember, we are talking about an image that the second beast tells the people of the earth to create. In essence, then, this man-made statue or image is brought to life by the second beast. It makes sense that he would have the people build or fashion the image because when he then brings it to life, they will marvel, since they know he had nothing to do with creating the image and therefore could not have done anything in secret to ensure that he would be able to bring it to life later.

But of course, what is difficult to know is whether the image is of the beast (empire) that has risen or whether this section of Scripture refers to the actual person who heads up the empire, the Antichrist.

Commentators – as can be expected – are in disagreement over this, with some believing that the beast that had received a fatal wound and then come back to life is the empire (Rome) while others believe it to be the Antichrist, who suffers a fatal wound but is resurrected. Certainly, the latter would be far more awe-inspiring and fantastic, and of course it would remind people of Jesus dying and coming back to life.

The idea of an empire dying out and coming back to life is certainly an acceptable interpretation as well, though admittedly not as awe-inspiring. Will people make the connection between the old Roman Empire and a newly risen version of the old Roman Empire? If the interpretation referencing the empire is valid, then there may be something that is not obvious related to the resurrection of that old empire.

We don't need to go into much of this because it doesn't add to our discussion here. Note that this second beast is very powerful and causes people to build an image of the first beast, then demands that they worship the first beast. Again, it is difficult to know if the second beast is pointing to some aspect of the old Roman Empire or the person of the Antichrist, who will rule over the Revised Roman Empire.

There is also speculation that this second beast is the Antichrist, but again, we don't need to delve into that because it takes us away from the point at hand. That is that the Roman Empire never truly dies, but merely goes through a number of major changes as it segues into its final form when the Antichrist will rule over a truly global empire.

Nonetheless, the second beast also makes it mandatory for all people to have his mark branded (tattooed?) on either their forehead or hand. For that to occur, this second beast has tremendous power.

Ultimately, God grants Satan his desire to have a final kingdom with a true global leader. This will afford Satan the opportunity to attempt to overthrow God Himself using every resource (natural and supernatural) at his disposal. Even with this, the Bible clearly tells us that Satan will fail.

Chapter 13
Character of the Fourth Empire

We learn many things about the end times from God's Word. We have some idea how the old Roman Empire appears to die, but essentially changes, morphs, and segues into a new form of that empire. The question might be asked, since we know who is going to ultimately lead this final phase of the fourth empire, what might the character of this final phase look like? Does Scripture tell us? I believe it does.

When I read the words of Paul to Timothy, in 2 Timothy 3:1-5, I understand what is being stated. But it is only when I begin to see how these things are exerting themselves throughout society that I begin to get a clear picture of exactly how bad things will be for us.

> *1 But realize this, that in the last days difficult times will come. 2 For men will be lovers of self, lovers of money, boastful, arrogant, revilers, disobedient to parents, ungrateful, unholy, 3 unloving, irreconcilable, malicious gossips, without self-control, brutal, haters of good, 4 treacherous, reckless, conceited, lovers of pleasure rather than lovers of God, 5 holding to a form of godliness, although they have denied its power; Avoid such men as these.*

The above text from Scripture certainly highlights the fact that people will be far different from what they were created to be. It's not until we begin to focus on each phrase or section that we begin to comprehend exactly what society will look like.

We also need to address what might have brought this attitude about, and it becomes clear that multiculturalism, born of political correctness, has done that. Political correctness has been a scourge on society.

Paul first warns his readers that difficult (terrible) times will come and then he describes what that will look like. Notice he is defining the times based on how people will act and react. The entire paragraph here is about what people will be like during the last days that will create terrible times for society.

Paul tells us that men will be lovers of self. If we take even a quick look at society, we will see that people are falling in love with themselves. They place their own wants/needs above the wants/needs of others. Paul is simply saying that above all things, people will become thoroughly selfish and self-centered. They won't care about how their actions affect others as long as they get what they want.

I'm sure all of us can think of examples that we are aware of or that have actually happened to us in which someone else did something so uncaring and selfish that it boggled our minds. We don't understand that type of callousness because it's not in us. Yet it appears to control the other person. It leaves us almost speechless because of the sheer audacity of his or her actions. How could a person treat someone else with such disdain, we ask? It is nothing less than a cold, hard-hearted callousness created by his or her self-love. This is the motivating factor for most of society and it is certainly becoming the norm.

Paul next states that people will be lovers of money. That is simply another form of selfishness. People will want money and things and they won't care how they get them, either. Over the last few months, more and more politicians have been caught red-handed with their hands in the cookie jar, taking what does not belong to them. They have been involved with illegal activities and thought they could get away with it.

But it's not just politicians. People who attend and/or work at churches have been caught as well. Recently, an associate pastor at a church in Texas was caught, having stolen over $250,000 from the church coffers over the space of two years. He is now seeking forgiveness and one can assume it's because he doesn't want to go to jail.[45]

What is going on with people? Selfishness. The problem with that word is that it really doesn't fully explain itself. We think of the selfishness of children as something they'll grow out of. The problem is that selfishness is where it all started with Adam and Eve. They decided that their understanding of the situation was better than God's,

---

[45] http://newsninja2012.com/houston-associate-pastor-steals-250k-from-church-over-two-years-seeking-forgiveness/ (3/29/2014)

and because Eve wanted the forbidden fruit, she found an excuse to take it, justifying herself for her actions.

Selfishness is the root of sin! It's where it all starts, and this is what people are becoming. They are throwing consciences out of the window and simply doing whatever they want because it pleases them. Consequences don't matter to these people. Hurting others does not matter. Getting wealthy by stealing or stepping on people doesn't matter as long as the goal is met.

The next three words in the text undergird the point Paul is making. He says people will become *boastful, arrogant,* and *revilers.* Today, people brag about everything. That bragging leads to an attitude of arrogance. That leads to becoming someone who reviles holy things.

In other words, these people have become so self-important that they see themselves as little gods. Isn't this what the New Age teaches anyway? You bet it does, and more and more people are buying that idea, because of what? It serves SELF.

Paul talks about something else that will motivate people in the last days. He says that people will become *disobedient to parents, ungrateful,* and *unholy.* That is all around us.

The government gives out freebies (entitlements) to people and those people begin to think that they are owed those things (as in reparations for slavery as one example). It is an attitude born of selfishness.

Look at this next list of adjectives used by Paul to describe people during the end times. He says: *unloving, irreconcilable, malicious gossips, without self-control, brutal, haters of good, treacherous, reckless, conceited, lovers of pleasure rather than lovers of God.*

Too many people love nothing but themselves today. They do not want to get along with others. In fact, they enjoy being at odds, being malicious. It serves SELF for them to castigate others because it puts them down. These people hate anything that does not serve their purposes. They are very brutal, they have no self-control, and they are treacherous, reckless, conceited, and live for pleasure.

This amazes me. In spite of everything that's happening in the world today, people live for pleasure. Though Rome burns, people dance the night away.

It is like the party Belshazzar threw for his people. They partied while Darius the Mede was just outside the walls of the city of Babylon with his troops. Belshazzar thought nothing of it because he firmly believed that Babylon was impenetrable. He was wrong and he was killed that very night. This is all recorded for us in Daniel 5. Please take time to read it.

This is the epitome of self-centeredness that makes people crave the limelight or causes them to do things that puff themselves up so that others will give them the type of adulation they so desperately want. It is a trap that ultimately causes the person to serve Satan because that is the very thing that causes his fall – pride.

Paul gives us direction at the end of verse five. He says simply, "avoid such men as these." The point is that while we can and should pray for them, we should give them a wide berth. There is nothing that we can say that will bring them down from their self-centered lofty height. If we get too close, there is a good chance we will get burned, so Paul essentially says leave them alone. Don't bother with them. Steer clear.

This is very good advice and something we obviously need to heed. Rather than get down to their level, stay where we are, pray for them and look for opportunities to witness to those who are open to the Gospel of Jesus.

With the onset of multiculturalism, selfishness has grown by leaps and bounds. Why is that? It's because of the fact that multiculturalism singles out specific cultures and winds up elevating them. While elevating some, others are denigrated.

This has been tragically happening not only in America, but in many countries throughout the world. It has produced the worst kind of fruit in which people are more loyal to "their own" than to all of humanity.

Multiculturalism has successfully pitted one race against another and it shows no sign of slowing down or reversing. In many cases, the race that is pushed to the bottom is the white race. As white liberals voice their concerns about what took place against blacks generations ago, these whites, while literally demonizing themselves, puff up blacks. The result is that whites are increasingly seen as the problem today, and the angst that many in minority communities feel is directed toward whites.

Multiculturalism is a bad thing because it is based on political correctness, something I've discussed in detail in two other books I wrote, *Falling Away* and *Caught in the Grip of Political Correctness*. I won't take the time to rehash what is discussed in those books, except to say that the basis for political correctness is decision-making that is based solely on *emotional virtue*, not absolute truth.

If something doesn't feel "right" or if it feels "wrong" then a decision is made based on that. It becomes social policy because those who do not agree with a particular line of reasoning are in danger of being called racist, homophobic, bigoted, and more. One can easily see how decisions based on emotional virtue are ever-changing.

One good example of this is the way NFL player Tim Tebow was treated on and off the field for the way he knelt. He was a Christian and wasn't afraid to let people know it. He was ridiculed by other players and by sports writers. There was no respect, no acceptance of Tim Tebow as a Christian.

Yet when a Dolphins NFL player is critical of another NFL player who happens to be gay, that Dolphins player is fined and sent for "educational training" because of something he tweeted.[46]

It's as one blogger noted, "*No doubt the NFL leaned on the Dolphins to hit Jones hard in the interest of sending a zero-tolerance message to the broader league, but like I said up top, I'm sure they didn't have to lean heavily.*"[47]

At the same time, "*People were grumbling on Twitter yesterday that even the slightest criticism of Sam for being gay is now verboten whereas it was A-OK to mock Tim Tebow for his faith, even on the field during the game.*"[48]

The author goes on to point out that it's a matter of economics because gay activists are well-positioned and well-funded. Christians, on the other hand, cannot equal that. Because of the financial power of the gay movement, companies do stand up and take notice. But in the end, it's really all part of the leftist agenda for America, to redefine and remake the culture – anything to move it away from those darn biblical values everyone on the left hates so much.

However, Christians are to make decisions based not on emotional virtue as those on the left do, but on absolute truth found in God's Word. Anything less is simply not truth.

We see the terrible situations throughout the globe that have arisen because of political correctness. I believe that ultimately, what Paul is describing in 2 Timothy 3 has to do with a foundation of political cor-

---

[46] http://hotair.com/archives/2014/05/12/dolphins-player-fined-sent-for-educational-training-after-tweet-about-michael-sam/ (5/12/2014)
[47] Ibid.
[48] Ibid.

rectness that allows and even forces people to make decisions based on emotional virtue. With this as the foundation, people can and do find all manner of excuses to do what they want, fully believing that those excuses make it right for them to be selfish, to be disobedient, to be brutal, to be lovers of money, etc.

Political Correctness is something the devil created because it stands in total opposition to God's World. It was very much alive during the time of Jesus and we see this when Pilate asked Jesus sarcastically, "What is truth?" (John 18:38). It was a rhetorical question. Pilate was not looking for a response because he did not believe that truth was absolute, but relative.

This relativity is what motivates much of society, and as people become more and more self-centered the toll it will take on society will be, in the final analysis, horrendous. I really don't think we can truly appreciate how bad it is going to get.

In the next chapter, I would like to provide even more details of how political correctness has created all forms of hatred in society. This fierceness is something that I believe will be one of the main characteristics of the final version of the Revised Roman Empire.

Chapter 14
EU Land & Sovereignty Grab

One of the things that has been part and parcel of the European Union (EU) is their gathering together of nations in Europe under the flag of the EU. When this occurs, not only does the EU become larger because of the land mass of the countries that are absorbed into the EU, but the national sovereignty of that newly absorbed country is essentially eradicated.

The flag itself *"consists of 12 golden stars in a circle on a blue background. The stars symbolise (sic) the ideals of unity, solidarity and harmony among the peoples of Europe. The number of stars has nothing to do with the number of member countries, though the circle is a symbol of unity."*[49]

---

[49] http://europa.eu/about-eu/basic-information/symbols/flag/index_en.htm (4/02/2014)

Yes, Spain, as part of the EU, is still called Spain. Italy is still called Italy. However, under the terms of the EU, the flag of each respective country flies beneath the flag of the EU. This is similar to the way the individual  states within the United States fly flags below the American flag. This practice has come to mean that the individual states in America are subservient to the federal government. This is not true. The federal government was created to actually serve the states, not dictate to them, but that's for another book.

In the case of the EU, a country that becomes part of that "empire" loses its sovereignty and must literally bow to the EU government. Though it began with only a few nations in 1951, it has grown to total 28 nations today in 2014 and continues to grow.

Ukraine is the latest country to try to work out a deal in order to come onboard with the EU, and because of it, Russia has gotten into the picture with roughly one hundred thousand troops ready to go to war over the issue. John Kerry – representing the US position (and that of the globalists) – wants Putin to back off. Putin, so far, appears unmovable.

But more has developed over this situation, and in fact, it would appear as though President Obama himself is talking up the EU as being good not only for European countries, but also for the United States. When we hear this type of talk, we need to understand who is really doing the talking. It's not President Obama. He is merely the mouthpiece (as is John Kerry). Yet we've also heard this same type of thing from previous presidents.

The real voices are in the shadows where they feel safe and secure. They are the globalists who are doing whatever they can to instill within the people of the world the idea that what the world needs is a one-world, one-company, globalized system that will supposedly "benefit" everyone. Of course, the "everyone" being referred to is the group of globalists themselves.

A number of informative articles (written as recently as April 2014) have highlighted this fact about President Obama wanting to partner with the EU, like one from the New American reporting on a meeting President Obama had with leaders of the EU March 26, 2014:

> *President Barack Obama and leaders of the European Union (EU) issued a Joint Statement at their March 26 meeting in Brussels declaring, among other things, their coordinated position on assistance to the Ukraine, as well as their continued flogging of the discredited 'climate change' alarmism, and commitment to conclude the Transatlantic Trade and Investment Partnership (TTIP) agreement between the EU and the United States.*[50]

Notice that President Obama has joined with EU leaders in agreeing that three things are very important that need to be accomplished:

1. Assisting Ukraine to become part of the EU
2. Continuing to push "climate change" lies, and
3. Putting TTIP into effect between the EU and the US

We've discussed the fact that the North American Free Trade Association (NAFTA[51]) was supposed to make it easier for products to go between the US, Canada, and Mexico. We've also mentioned the fact that the North American Union (NAU) was something that was/is

---

[50] http://www.thenewamerican.com/usnews/foreign-policy/item/17962-obama-froman-use-ukraine-to-push-us-eu-merger (4/02/2014)
[51] http://en.wikipedia.org/wiki/North_American_Free_Trade_Agreement (4/02/2014)

supposed to unite these three countries in an economic and political "union."[52]

It's possible that these things are still on the table, but we now see that President Obama is aligning himself with the EU and their purposes. The truth is that – as I've stated – the Global Elite (GE) really needs to create groups of countries. This removes sovereignty from those countries and gives the globalists greater control.

Once the globalists have that control, they can then work to create larger groupings of countries as they create their one-world paradise. Interestingly enough, the Club of Rome[53] (one of those secret societies) has done at least some of the legwork by creating a document that divides the world up into ten parts. Dr. John Coleman has written a short, concise book on the development and purpose of this "club." It's called *The Club of Rome*, published in 2010.

You'll recall the ten horns of Revelation 13. Once the world is fully united, it can be managed by one "king" for each of the ten sections. Though separated into sections, the world will still be one in purpose and direction.

The Club of Rome has produced numerous resources that show their intentions. One two-page PDF summarizes their goals in *"The Programme of the Club of Rome on A New Path for World Development."*[54]

The five broad goals are:

1. *Environment and Resources:*
    a. *Climate Change, Energy Security, Ecosystems and Water.*
2. *Globalisation:* (sic)

---

[52] http://en.wikipedia.org/wiki/North_American_Union (3/02/2014)
[53] http://en.wikipedia.org/wiki/Club_of_Rome (4/02/2014)
[54] http://clubofrome.org/cms/wp-content/uploads/2011/07/CoR_Flyer_090605.pdf (4/02/2014)

a. *Distribution of Wealth and Income, Employment, Economic Restructuring, Trade and Finance.*
3. International Development:
   a. *Demographic Growth, Environmental Stress, Poverty, Food Production, Health and Employment.*
4. Social Transformation:
   a. *Social Change, Values, Culture, Identity and Behaviour (sic)*
5. Peace and Security:
   a. *Justice, Democracy, Governance, Solidarity, Security and Peace.*

What we clearly have are people who believe they know what's best for the entire globe and are actually working to bring it about. The fact that they have divided the world into ten sections should also not come as a surprise.

But the astounding thing is that this group has done this; they have gotten together and discussed what they think is best for the world based on their (Global Elite's) needs and wants. It is the height of hubris, yet isn't that one of the traits of all dictators? Shown on the map below is how they have broken up the world according to a document the group released in 1974 titled *"Regionalized and Adaptive Model of the Global World System."*[55]

This is how the Global Elite think. For them, there is no God because they are god. They believe they were put here to rule people and the world itself. To that end, they seek to move mountains and realign the globe to their liking.

Notice that in the map below, North America is one grouping. All of South America is another. District number two represents the EU in expanded form and so on. To them, this is the United World, simply

---

[55] http://conspiracywiki.com/documents/club-of-rome-report-regionalized-and-adaptive-model-of-the-global-world.pdf (4/02/2014)

broken down (on paper) into ten manageable sections, allowing the globalists to rule in a way that spreads the wealth of rulership, so to speak, so that ten of the top globalists will actually rule the entire world.

What they are not banking on, of course, is the fact that the Antichrist will rise up from among them and gain full control of the world government that the globalists have worked so hard to create. They won't see that coming at all simply because they don't read the Bible or care what it says.

Getting back to the article quoted from earlier, President Obama, in his push to support the EU, stated, *"Europe, including the European Union, is the cornerstone of our engagement around the world. We are*

Ten Divisions of New World by Club of Rome (1973)

Regions:

1. North America
2. Western Europe
3. Japan
4. Australia and South Africa
5. Eastern Europe
6. Latin America
7. North Africa and the Middle East
8. Main Africa
9. South and Southeast Asia
10. Centrally Planned Asia

more secure and we are more prosperous, the world is safer and more just, when Europe and America stand as one."[56] This is the false reality that globalists tout and want us to believe wholeheartedly. Most of us reading that statement would recognize it as a complete lie.

Look carefully at the wording, though. President Obama says that the EU is the "cornerstone of our engagement around the world." What can this possibly mean other than the fact that President Obama is aligning himself with the goals and policies of the EU for America? At the same time, why can't the United States have its own power and engagement around the world? We certainly used to have such presence, but that is being torn away.

The same article also noted that *"The Joint Statement also reiterated support for the World Trade Organization and the United Nations, as well as support for UN/NATO military intervention in Africa, and implementation of various disarmament treaties, including the UN Arms Trade Treaty that targets the Second Amendment and the rights of individual U.S. citizens to keep and bear firearms."*[57]

This is not only extremely problematic for the United States, but in actuality, it is absolutely treasonous because Mr. Obama is stating that he is willing to do what is necessary to bring the United States into alignment with the goals of the EU, the UN, NATO, and the WTO. This is not what is meant when a president takes the oath of office to protect and uphold the United States Constitution. This is what a liar, thief, and corrupt politician does who is actually working for the Global Elite and not the American people.

The tragedy here is that things are quickly moving toward this end. There is a great deal that is going on and a good portion of it is no longer done completely in the shadows, but right in front of our nos-

---

[56] http://www.thenewamerican.com/usnews/foreign-policy/item/17962-obama-froman-use-ukraine-to-push-us-eu-merger (4/02/2014)
[57] Ibid.

es. This means that the Global Elite now believe themselves to be unstoppable. They have gained enough momentum that the momentum alone thwarts those who try to change what is coming.

The article further declares a number of things: *"Several days before President Obama headed to Brussels, his point man on the TTIP, U.S. Trade Representative Michael Froman...said that he wants a trans-Atlantic trade deal to be as strong as the longstanding NATO alliance between the United States and Europe, 'We want for TTIP [Transatlantic Trade and Investment Partnership] to help build an economic and a trade relationship that is as strong as the strongest military alliance in the world, but fundamentally it has to be driven by the underlying economics'."*[58]

The meaning of Froman's words has tremendous implications. *"In announcing his desire to craft a TTIP that would be the equivalent of an economic NATO, Froman was not speaking only (or even primarily) for the Obama White House, but also for Pratt House, the headquarters of the Council on Foreign Relations (CFR), the globalist brain trust that has been the guiding subversive force behind U.S. administrations (both Democrat and Republican) for much of the past century."*[59]

The Council on Foreign Relations (CFR) has long been considered a group think-tank with one purpose – undermining US foreign policy as outlined within the Constitution. The aim is to replace the Constitution with policies that are sought after by the GE, so that they and they alone benefit.

As we have stated, it almost seems like the EU's main purpose is to subvert the sovereignty of individual nations. Certainly, this is the major outcome for every nation that joins the EU.

---

[58] http://www.thenewamerican.com/usnews/foreign-policy/item/17962-obama-froman-use-ukraine-to-push-us-eu-merger (4/02/2014)
[59] Ibid.

The concept of creating a TTIP between the EU and the US has been in the works for some time, going back at least to April of 2013. The major problem with the attempts to create this TTIP is that it is diversionary and dishonest. *"They are publicly packaging and promoting the agreements as 'trade agreements' when, in fact, they have been designed as evolving projects that will progressively 'integrate' the economies and political systems of the signatory nations into a supranational regime modeled along the lines of the European Union."*[60]

The idea of having a supranational regime is the major goal because it means any company that the Global Elite creates will have no national boundaries to worry about. They want their one-world company to run smoothly without worrying about taxes, tariffs, or anything else. Unions won't exist either, but of course union bosses have no clue that's what's coming. They're being used now to achieve the goals of the Elite, but once those goals are achieved, does anyone really believe that the unions will exist any longer?

Another article that sheds further light on this subject is by Dennis Behreandt, called "Translantic Two-Step."[61] This particular article goes back a number of years to the presidency of George W. Bush (April 2007). The article *"details the efforts of globalist elites in organizations such as the Council on Foreign Relations, the Transatlantic Policy Network, the Brookings Institution, the Carnegie Endowment for International Peace, and others, to use the battering ram of trade agreements to smuggle political and economic integration schemes that are aimed at destroying national sovereignty."*[62]

---

[60] http://www.thenewamerican.com/usnews/foreign-policy/item/15185-cfr-applauds-european-union-s-real-subversion-of-sovereignty (4/02/2014)
[61] http://www.thenewamerican.com/usnews/foreign-policy/item/1151-transatlantic-two-step (4/02/2014)
[62] http://www.thenewamerican.com/usnews/foreign-policy/item/15185-cfr-applauds-european-union-s-real-subversion-of-sovereignty (5/12/2014)

People need to realize that it really doesn't matter who sits in the Oval Office because no one – Republican or Democrat – gets to become president without the approval of the Global Elite. That's simply the way it is in America and it's been that way for over 100 years.

Each president takes up the cause of the Elite. It's their job not to serve the best interests of the people of the United States or uphold and protect the US Constitution. Without the loyalty of each US president, the GE could not have made such gains. Any president (or other elected official) who chooses not to follow dictates of the Elite will either not remain in office long or end up dead.

Many tend to think that George W. Bush was a decent president, yet he gave us the so-called Patriot Act, which was said to make the people of America safer. That act gave birth to the Department of Homeland Security (DHS), and so far all it's done is spent millions upon millions of dollars and chipped away at the Fourth Amendment nonstop.

Not once (that anyone knows of) has the DHS actually caught a terrorist before he got on an airplane. Yet more security features are implemented, further removing rights of Americans without due process.

Beyond implementing freedom-robbing programs like DHS via the Patriot Act, however, President Bush has clearly worked with the Elitists to help bring about a one-world order. This new order (also advocated by Bush Sr.) is seen in its ties with the EU. In a way, though, this is all smoke and mirrors because the absolute goal of the Elites is to put themselves in charge of the globe.

President Bush stated some things regarding TTIP that should cause alarm for every freedom-loving American. Here's what he said:

> *I told the chancellor and the president that the EU-U.S. relations are very important to our country...that not only is it important*

for us to strategize how to promote prosperity and peace, but it's important for us to achieve concrete results. And we have done so. I thank the chancellor and Jos very much for the trans-Atlantic economic integration plan that the three of us signed today. It is a statement of the importance of trade. It is a commitment to eliminating barriers to trade. It is a recognition that the closer that the United States and the EU become, the better off our people become. So this is a substantial agreement and I appreciate it.[63]

It's obvious that this idea that the US working with the EU creates a better situation for the US is not only not true, but asinine. It will mean a loss of sovereignty of US powers to the EU.

It appears as though the Revised Roman Empire is taking shape and is further along than most of us would like to admit. The EU is the favored empire of the UN because the EU supports all of the goals of the UN, including disarmament.

The more control the EU gains over sovereign nations, the more sovereignty those nations will lose. Even though President Bush discussed back in 2007 what was essentially a US merger with the EU, there was barely a blip on the news radar over it. *"What seems like a revolutionary step toward transatlantic merger was little remarked in the press."*[64]

What type of proof beyond this do we need to know that the Elites also control the press? There is far more truth on the Internet than can be gained from the various TV, radio, and newspaper news outlets. Yet, even here, the idea that is often sarcastically stated, "if it's

---

[63] http://www.thenewamerican.com/usnews/foreign-policy/item/15185-cfr-applauds-european-union-s-real-subversion-of-sovereignty (4/02/2014)
[64] http://www.thenewamerican.com/usnews/foreign-policy/item/1151-transatlantic-two-step (4/02/2014)

on the Internet, it must be true," is very likely stated to make people doubt the veracity of information on the Net.

Granted, some of the information on the Net is questionable at best. It's probably placed there to throw people off the track from truth. Care needs to be taken when researching anything because if articles are not heavily sourced, there is reason to question them. Even with that, care should be taken.

The more I have researched this via Scripture and the things that are happening in society, the more clearly it appears that the world is moving toward a one-world system. There is simply too much information available that tends to prove these things. The history of the Rockefellers in America, the many groups and agencies they've created to help overthrow the United States Constitution, as well as the many groups that have been created by other globalists all point to a one-world system.

Why do we have so many on the far left doing whatever they can to bring the United States under the so-called sovereignty of the UN? Why is there such a firm belief that the US needs to somehow merge with the EU?

Why is there so much happening in today's US Congress that shows politician after politician doing all they can to subvert the Constitution? It's not a small handful of them either. It appears to be a majority of individuals who have been elected to office and who seem to believe that their job is to overthrow the Constitution in order to change the fabric of the United States.

Why do so many politicians seem to be completely oblivious to the fact that America is a Constitutional Republic and not a Democracy? The amount of ignorance is absolutely astounding, yet it continues, propped up by the media and others from the left. It's promoted by political correctness and allowed to grow because of it.

There are many reasons for it, and it certainly seems like American society is being thoroughly overwhelmed by all the forces that are attempting to remake it. The Bible says that the world will become one. We are seeing it happen.

Chapter 15
Genocide is Part of the Plan

There is much that has been written regarding what is being called the genocide of South Africa whites. You may be ahead of me in that regard. The white farmers – called the "Boers" – have been (and continue to be) murdered over the last several years because African National Congress (ANC), which is the ruling party, wants all the farmland that whites currently own. One African white farmer has stated succinctly, *"It's politically correct to kill whites these days."*[65]

In July of 2012, Dr. Gregory Stanton, head of the nonprofit group Genocide Watch, conducted a fact-finding mission in

---

[65] http://whitegenocideproject.com/genocide-watch-urges-white-afrikaners-to-flee-south-africa/ (3/29/2014)

South Africa. He concluded that there is a coordinated campaign of genocide being conducted against white farmers, known as Boers. "The farm murders, we have become convinced, are not accidental," Stanton contended. "It was very clear that the massacres were not common crimes," he added—especially because of the absolute barbarity used against the victims. "We don't know exactly who is planning them yet, but what we are calling for is an international investigation," he added.

The number of farm murders, or "plaasmoorde" as it is called in Afrikaans, is staggering. Over the last decade, it is estimated that at least 3000 Boers have been killed.[66]

South Africa's black government has come under fire (much the way the previous white government did) because of the amount of racism that has been ignored and even incited against whites. It got so bad in 2008, the South Africa government stopped keeping track of all the many white farmers being murdered. All too often, these murders – though absolutely barbaric (including torture, rape, and more) – were simply listed as "accidents" or related to "robberies" gone bad.

One individual – author Adriana Stuijt (Twitter: @AdrianaStuijt) – has done numerous reports on the situation and has stated that when the government stopped counting back in 2008, the number of black on white murders had already reached 85,000. If we stop to consider this, that is a huge number, which equals a terrible tragedy.

But in many ways, this appears to be a *planned* tragedy. Many attest that the South Africa government has been actually supporting and even inciting attacks against white farmers. When South Africa cele-

---

[66] http://whitegenocideproject.com/genocide-watch-urges-white-afrikaners-to-flee-south-africa/ (3/29/2014)

brated the 100th year of the ANC, the president – Zuma – joined in the singing of the song with the line, "*Shoot the Boer.*"

One of the biggest names connected to South Africa is Nelson Mandela, who died not long ago (December 2013). The world tends to hold him up as someone who, like Ghandi, worked through peaceful methods to overturn the racism propagated by the then white government. However, the truth may be far different.

> *Mandela advocated violent resistance against the apartheid government. When people say that Mandela 'fought' for equality, they mean it literally. His victory against apartheid took a very different path than Gandhi's.*[67]

Eventually, Mandela helped found the para-military arm of the ANC "*called Umkhonto we Sizwe or 'Spear of the Nation.' The group committed sabotage against state buildings and infrastructure. He explained at his 1964 trial that peaceful efforts had failed; 'only then did we decide to answer violence with violence'.*"[68]

Mandela was originally sentenced to life in prison. In 1985, he was offered freedom if he would simply swear to never use violence. He refused, but was ultimately freed in 1990, with apartheid ending in 1991. In 1994, the first election was held allowing blacks to vote and Mandela was elected president.

Interestingly enough, in the 1980s, Mandela's ANC was "*placed on America's official list of terrorist groups.*" He was known for criticizing the Iraq war and sided with Saddam Hussein. The National Review stated then that *"his vicious anti-Americanism and support for Saddam*

---

[67] http://freedomoutpost.com/2013/12/nelson-mandela-media-fawns-though-marxist-terrorist/ (3/29/2014)
[68] Ibid.

Hussein should come as no surprise, given his longstanding dedication to communism and praise for terrorists."[69]

Rumors have continued that Mandela was at the least a communist sympathizer. That may be due to the fact that, "*In South Africa, it was the Soviet bloc—the same communist governments that were brutally repressing their own people—that helped the ANC fight apartheid.*"[70]

> *South Africa is about 40 years ahead of majority White countries, in terms of 'anti-racism'. As we can see, first it starts with millions of non-Whites being encouraged into a White country; then comes the forced assimilation of said immigrants; then finally, when Whites become a minority it ends up much like South Africa...a system that turns against White people and*

---

[69] http://www.thedailybeast.com/articles/2013/12/05/don-t-sanitize-nelson-mandela-he-s-honored-now-but-was-hated-then.html (3/29/2014)
[70] http://freedomoutpost.com/2013/12/nelson-mandela-media-fawns-though-marxist-terrorist/ (3/29/2014)

> *ONLY White people in an attempt to wipe them out – genocide.*[71]

It would appear that maybe there is more to the growing movement of racism within the United States as well. We see it on an increasingly large scale and it goes all the way to the highest offices in the land. President Obama came out in defense of Trayvon Martin.[72] Eric Holder's DOJ has done everything it can to support blacks even when they have broken the law,[73] as in the case of the New Black Panther members who had been tried and convicted with respect to their antics outside a polling precinct in Philly. They were never sentenced and their case just seemed to disappear.

The many cases of black on white crime where whites are severely injured or killed are rarely, if ever, charged as hate crimes. Yet, this is almost always the case when the races are reversed.

What has been happening in South Africa has been described as *"post-racial,"* *"anti-racism,"* or *"post-white."* Apparently, white farmers in South Africa have come to understand that this is the real goal of any *anti-racism* campaign.

The above quote outlines how it happens.

1. Non-Whites are encouraged into a white country
2. Forced assimilation of those immigrants
3. Whites become the minority
4. System turns against whites

---

[71] http://freedomoutpost.com/2013/12/nelson-mandela-media-fawns-though-marxist-terrorist/ (3/29/2014).
[72] http://freedomoutpost.com/2013/07/barack-obama-honor-travon-martin-with-more-gun-control/ (3/29/2014)
[73] http://freedomoutpost.com/2013/07/eric-holders-justice-department-promulgates-racism-via-thomas-perez-hud/ (3/29/2014)

This is what has happened in South Africa, and we have seen many Africans over the last several decades immigrating to other countries, countries like Great Britain, Italy, the Netherlands, and the United States. What do we see in these countries today? Great Britain is in upheaval, and the Netherlands has been and continues reeling from the things that have occurred there.

Here in the United States, it seems that our government has been deliberately bringing in as many non-whites as possible, and they are immediately placed on public assistance. The doors are thrown open wide for them. Meanwhile, our government is doing what it can to shut down one business after another.

There are also many Hispanic leaders who have stated racist ideals, directed at white people. Interestingly enough, Snopes uses an entire page to highlight many of these quotable quotes.[74] While Snopes is not a source that I normally run to, in this case at least they have presented a decent amount of information that can be verified by other sources.

This reactionary position that is touted by the left, accepted by the media, and spread among minorities is the result of a Global Elite that wants change through societal unrest and disobedience. They'll take it any way they can get it, even brainwashing people into thinking that killing whites is the solution that must be utilized.

I used to think that the government wanted to take our guns away so that we couldn't resist the government. I still think that's true, but I am now realizing – based on the process that's unfolded in South Africa – that there is another reason to remove our guns. It will certainly make whites defenseless. In South Africa, the government has been working hard to make it impossible for white farmers to own guns.

---

[74] http://www.snopes.com/politics/quotes/hispanicleaders.asp (3/29/2014)

This makes them defenseless against marauding groups of ANC-empowered blacks.

In America, society has changed very quickly in the past eight to ten years. It's not just lawlessness that seems to abound. It's lawlessness with a vengeance and purpose. It is designed to take whites (as well as conservative minorities) out of the picture entirely.

The troubling thing about what I just said in this chapter is that while some will accuse me of fomenting racism, these same people will find no fault in the words of Professor Jose Angel Gutierrez and many others like him who really do want all white people dead. When you hear the phrase "anti-racist," it is code for "anti-white."

During a Red October Campaign march to make the problem of South African white genocide known, one individual said, "*Seventeen of our people are murdered every month by a black person. Now I can only imagine the international outcry if 17 black people a month were murdered by a white person."*[75]

Then we have the quote from an individual who used to teach at the college level, Dr. Kamau Kambon (pictured above). His comment pretty much sums up what the "*anti-racist*" movement is all about. His website is designed to solve what he calls "the problem" and continue to work toward African liberation (from white rule). The problem with this is that in the process, white genocide is occurring at an alarming rate and people like Kambon simply don't care because they only care for "their people."

"And then finally I want to say that we need one idea, and we're not thinking about a solution to the problem ... And the one idea is, how we are going to exterminate White people because that in my estimation is the only conclusion I have come to. We have to exterminate white people off the face of the planet,"[76] - Kamau Kambon[77], former professor of African-American Studies.

Think this is all garbage? Think it's overstated and created by insecure whites afraid of the bogey man? Then research it. Start at the Truth About South Africa website.[78]

Aside from political correctness, much of this type of thinking is made possible by something called Critical Race Theory, which is a subject I dealt with in two of my previous books, *Falling Away* and *Caught in the Grip of Political Correctness*. In essence, Critical Race Theory, largely connected to deceased educator Derrick Bell, surmises that white people enjoy "white privilege" solely for being white.

---

[75] http://www.enca.com/south-africa/red-october-plight-whites-new-south-africa (3/29/2014)
[76] http://whitegenocideproject.com/what-anti-whites-say/ (3/29/2014)
[77] http://www.kamaukambon.org/ (3/29/2014)
[78] http://www.thetruthaboutsouthafrica.com/p/white-genocide-in-south-africa.html (3/29/2014)

This theory has never been proven but is widely accepted among minorities. Because "white privilege" is something that is assumed to be true, many minorities ignore the actual situation, preferring to believe that white people automatically have a leg up in society and receive special privileges that blacks and other minorities don't.

The problem with this is that all one has to do is look at the numbers of people employed by the government and the reality quickly becomes apparent. But as long as people believe that whites gain privileges just for being white, then the truth will never be seen.

Critical Race Theory even goes so far as to say that whites, while not intentionally doing things that put them in the privileged positions, are still on the receiving end of privileges, often without even realizing it. However, when we look at the scholarships available for many colleges, more often than not, whites are excluded.

In Congress, there is every color of the rainbow in special caucus groups, including, most recently, the Islamic Caucus. However, there is no white caucus because that would be seen as racist. Everyone else can have one, but not whites, based on the errant and unproven belief that whites, by simply being white, have access to privileges that others don't.

However, it is this type of attitude and belief about society and how it works that goes a long way in fomenting problems between the races. Add to that the daily bantering of race-baiting talking heads who continue to pound into minorities that they aren't getting a fair shake, and it's not long before people within those minorities begin to believe what they're being told.

Imagine if someone from the white community stood up and said what Robert Mugabe or Kamau Kambon has stated. There would be an immediate cry of racism from the left, and rightly so. These comments are not something that intelligent people of civilized worlds should say, believe, or advocate. Yet, they do say them and they get away with saying them because of political correctness.

When taken together, there are many things that are causing society to look exactly like Paul's description in 2 Timothy 3. We are quickly becoming a global society of individuals who only care about themselves, their own needs, and the needs of their "people." This is also another false idea. Blacks and other minorities want the world to believe that in their particular community, it's one for all and all for one. This is not reality, but minorities do not want the world to know it's not reality.

This is why the black community will come together in support of Trayvon Martin even before all the facts are out. When a black person comes out saying he wouldn't support Trayvon Martin simply because he's black (as Kobe Bryant recently did), others from the black community will make public statements condemning his words.[79]

This is exactly what happens when a black person "comes out" as a conservative and actually votes Republican. Since most blacks vote Democrat, the idea is that all blacks are supposed to stick together and see things the same way. No one group is filled with people who all think the same, but blacks want us to believe that this is case, so they castigate and ostracize those blacks who don't toe the line.

This is exactly what occurred with Ebony's senior editor, Jamilah Lemieux, referring to Juan Williams' son as a "white dude."[80] While an apology was eventually issued by the magazine, this type of de-

---

[79] http://www.theblaze.com/stories/2014/03/27/kobe-bryant-incurs-wrath-of-the-left-over-his-comments-on-trayvon-martin-case/ (3/29/2014)
[80] http://newsninja2012.com/ebony-magazine-staffer-jamilah-lemieux-racially-attacks-rnc-raffi-williams-here-comes-a-white-dude-via-twitter/ (3/29/2014)

meanor by blacks toward other blacks who are not Democrats and/or liberal is par for the course.

Again though, all of this points to the fact that society is fractionalizing. It is doing so because before the world can come together as "one," I believe the Global Elite first needs to pull it apart. Crises – one after another – make this happen, and angst from one culture or race to another can also accomplish it. In fact, I fully believe that the Global Elite has been working all ends against the middle, doing everything they can to create havoc in society. A society that is splintering is a society that can be molded. When things are fine, this is not easy to do, to say the least.

Could this be why there have been so many wars throughout history? Yes. Could it be why even the threat of war is something that can create problems in society? Yes, absolutely. In fact, in His Olivet Discourse (Matthew 24), Jesus spoke of wars and rumors of wars.

In Daniel 9:24-27, note that there are three sections of "weeks" referenced. The first is seven "weeks," immediately followed by sixty-two "weeks." After this second set of "weeks," (the 62), there is a bit of a break. The text specifically says in verse 26:

> *Then after the sixty-two weeks the Messiah will be cut off and have nothing, and the people of the prince who is to come will destroy the city and the sanctuary. And its end will come with a flood;* **even to the end there will be war**; *desolations are determined.*

The section in bold highlights the fact that until the end of this age, there will be wars. War is not going to go away. It's one of the best things the Global Elite can play with in order to increase frustration, fear, angst, and more. Wars also do two other things, both of which the Global Elite want to happen. When war happens, people die. As far as the Elite are concerned, this is a good thing because it reduces the population.

Another thing that happens with war is that the Elite make lots of money because their companies are the ones who produce the tanks, the planes, the munitions that are used in war. The Elite do not care which side they sell them to, either. They simply want to sell them to make money, and make money they do.

In truth, whether it's war, plagues (natural or man-made), race wars, civil wars, or what have you, the Global Elite benefit because they come that much closer to a full breakdown in global society. Once that happens, they will then come in with the solutions. Of course, everyone will need to cooperate and be willing to give up more of their "rights," but people are willing to do that.

We've seen that repeatedly with the Patriot Act (which gave birth to the Department of Homeland Security), the restriction of our Fourth Amendment rights, all done in the name of "keeping the public safe." It's the same with the Second Amendment rights that the federal government continues to whittle away at. They're no more interested in keeping the public safe than Satan wants people to become saved.

The government is too often used by the Global Elite to manifest their goals and there really is no end in sight. Paul's words in 2 Timothy 3 speaks of just how terrible and deadly society will become toward the end. I firmly believe that this is what we are seeing in society now.

Society has changed drastically since I was a kid and even since I was a young adult. Today, people are brasher, ruder, more crude, and in general, far more superficial and mean-spirited.

This is the result of people who have become exceedingly selfish and unable to sympathize or empathize with others. It speaks of just how terrible it will be if this is what it is now.

The Revised Roman Empire will be tremendously harsh in its final stage, leading up to the time of Christ's physical return. Is it any wonder that the apostle John was frightened when he saw the final form of the fourth beast from God's perspective? I'm sure it was not a pretty sight, and compared to what's going on in civilization now, we know that we are well on our way.

The old Roman Empire appeared to die. Many historians will tell you that the empire died during the AD 400s. Yet, if we look closely, we can see that it really didn't die, but changed into other venues.

The eastern leg of the old Roman Empire went through the Byzantine Empire, then Constantine ruled, and then the Ottoman Empire took over from there. Though the Ottoman Empire went away, Islam did not and still exists today with a vengeance. In fact, the spread of Islam appears to be picking up speed as it moves from one country to the next.

The western leg was taken over by Germanic tribes, which then gave way to Charlemagne in what eventually became known as the Holy Roman Empire. Eventually, this gave way to the European Union, which is what exists today.

Surely, the Roman Empire didn't really die. It has morphed into something else completely and appears ready to burst onto the global community in its final form. It is destined to happen because the Bible says it will.

One thing we need to remember is that all of this happens because God has either decreed it or allowed it. He has done so for His own purposes, chief of which is that He will be glorified by everything that occurs in the universe He created.

As hard as Satan may try to overcome Him and as much as human beings want to ignore Him, He will not be ignored. Satan will not prevail. Christian, hold on to that!

Chapter 16
The Elite's Future Dreams

To hear Jacques Attali tell it, the future is looking very bright...for the Global Elite (GE), that is. Attali published a book in 2006[81] that covers a great deal of what the GE is planning on bringing to fulfillment. Since the GE see themselves as individuals who were put here on this earth to rule the peons (that would be you and me), the plans that Attali outlines are simply par for the course.

Writer David Richards comments on Attali's background and credentials: *"Attali is a high-level technocrat working to fulfill the New World Order."*[82] Richards further notes,

---

[81] The book also lists 2011 as a publishing date, possibly indicating the book was updated in 2011
[82] http://www.henrymakow.com/attali.html#sthash.Js6cFQum.dpuf (4/08/2014)

> *Jacques Attali has a varied CV. For ten years he worked as an adviser to former French President Francois Mitterrand. In 1980, he started the European program Eurêka (a major European program on new technologies that invented, among other things, the MP3).*
>
> *In 1991, he co-founded the European Bank for Reconstruction and Development. He is also at the origin of the higher education reform, known as LMD, designed to bring all European degrees into line.*

When Attali's book was published, the cover included three words from Henry Kissinger: *Brilliant and provocative.* Knowing this is coming from an individual like Kissinger who has been associated with the GE for decades, we immediately understand where Attali is coming from. I mean, gee whiz, it's "brilliant" and "provocative" because it paints such a rosy picture of the future for the privileged few while presenting a dire one for those outside that group.

The book itself (translated into English by Jeremy Leggatt) includes 6 chapters totaling just over 290 pages. The individual chapter titles are as follows:

1. A Very Long History
2. A Brief History of Capitalism
3. The End of the American Empire
4. First Wave of the Future: Planetary Empire
5. Second Wave of the Future: Planetary War
6. Third Wave of the Future: Planetary Democracy

This chapter is not so much a review of Attali's book but simply provides the cogent points he makes. This helps us understand not only where the GE is leading us, but it highlights the risks involved as well.

Let's skip ahead to chapter three, which deals with the end of America's Empire. Much of what Attali states simply points us in the direction of the GE. In fact, Attali appears to be little more than a "voice crying in the wilderness" for them. Attali states,

> *From generation to generation, [economic evolution] spreads individual freedom and channels desires toward their mercantile end. From century to century, farmers have migrated into cities. From century to century, the forces of market democracy have coalesced into an ever-growing and more integrated market around a temporary core. To assume power over the mercantile world – to become its core – a city or region must be the biggest communication center of its day, and must be endowed with a very powerful agricultural and industrialized hinterland. This core must also be capable of creating banking institutions bold enough to finance the plans of an innovative class, putting new technologies to work, allowing the transformation of the most daunting services into industrial objects. And finally, the core must be able to exert political, social, cultural, and military control over hostile minorities, lines of communication, and sources of raw materials.*[83]

Yes, that was a mouthful; however, note what he truly says in that paragraph. He says that over time, things are channeled toward a market democracy that continues to grow through integration. This is the core. In order to build, maintain, and direct this core, it takes a huge central system, built by "an innovative class" of people (think: Global Elite) who know how to make it work.

Probably the most important thought is the last sentence. This group of individuals who have created this core (and sustain it as well) must be powerful enough to exert the kind of political, social, cultural, and military pressure to keep "hostile minorities" from bringing it

---

[83] Jacques Attali, *A Brief History of the Future* (2006), p. 105

down. His reference to "hostile minorities" does not mean "blacks," "browns," or some other ethnic minority. He is stating that anyone who opposes the work of the "innovative class" of people who put together the core of tomorrow is the "hostile minority," and every effort will be made to put them down.

What is fascinating, of course, is that Attali constantly speaks of "capitalism" as though it's not the enemy. Yet we've experienced and witnessed protests by people who call themselves the 99%, or those who made up the Occupy Movement. This group protested against the "bad" companies like Wall Street stock brokers and capitalism in general as being evil. It's evil because it makes the rich richer by stepping on the perceived little guy.

We hear a lot of talk now with President Obama and his desire to spread the wealth. Numerous articles and books have been written on President Obama's stated desire to do what has become known as the Obama rule. *"Taxes must be high simply to spread the wealth, never mind the impact on the economy or government revenue. It's all about 'fairness,' baby."*[84]

This whole concept is based on socialism and the only people who deny that are those on the left. But why is there such a push for what appears to be socialism, if Attali speaks of capitalism in a way that makes us believe that without the restrictions currently placed on capitalism, it would run even smoother?

> *But the current form of capitalism lives under the same threats as those that finished off previous forms. Its security imperiled, its innovative class can no longer be trusted, industrially promising technical progress is slower and slower, and financial speculation is out of control. Disparities worsen, anger rumbles, and deep indebtedness piles*

---

[84] http://www.realclearpolitics.com/2012/04/11/the_obama_rule_spread_the_wealth_around_277410.html (4/08/2014)

> *up. Most disturbing of all is the flagging of the core's will to persevere at the top.*[85]

Note that Attali indicates that the current form of capitalism exists under the same set of rules that eliminated previous forms of it. In order to avoid the same result, something must be done. He speaks as though he were a man "in the know" about what was going on behind the scenes. He speaks of the 2008 election of Obama, and regarding the European Union, he notes, *"During these next two decades, the European Union will probably be no more than a simple common economic space, enlarged to include the former Yugoslavia, Bulgaria, Moldova, and Ukraine."* Again, even if this book was updated in 2011, I find it interesting that as I write this chapter, Ukraine is undergoing quite a bit of upheaval with Putin taking Crimea as part of Russia and willing to fight to gain a hold on Ukraine as well. The USA (and UN) vows to resist Putin's efforts, and so far war has not broken out.

Attali has some other "predictions" in his book and one can only wonder how he came up with them. This is a rhetorical question, of course, because of Attali's known ties to many within the GE.

In his article, writer David Richards indicates that Attali believes this century will unfold in several ways:

1. *Super-empire = an era of privatization where corporations rule the day. He writes, "money will finally rid itself of everything that threatens it - including nation states, which it will progressively dismantle." The market will become the world's only recognized law. A system of power whose 'structures remain elusive but whose goal is global.'*
2. *Hyperconflict = super-empire will implode and there will be a period of worldwide chaos. Starting about 2030, Attali foresees*

---

[85] Jacques Attali, *A Brief History of the Future* (2006), p. 106

> *'devastating wars, pitting nations, religious groups, terrorist entities, and free-market pirates against one another'.*
> 3. *Hyperdemocracy (2060) = Exhausted by wars and social upheavals the world public will welcome with open arms 'the creation of a democratic world government.' It will be a collectivist system, with everyone working towards the 'common good.'*[86]

Richards has – in a nutshell – explained in what direction the world will move according to Attali. When we look specifically at what others have written about the coming global system that is being put into place now, it becomes clear that this global system is fully based around a one-world company (as Dennis Cuddy refers to it), but will also involve a one-world government. This one-world government will undoubtedly be linked to the UN (as enforcer[87]) or have the UN as its core and will ensure that the one-world company runs smoothly.

Regarding these concepts, Cuddy states, "*While the ultimate goal of the global elite is a World Socialist Government resulting from a dialectical process, what we have recently experienced is perhaps best characterized as 'multinational corporatism'.*"[88]

Cuddy further pronounces, "*As this global system breaks down national economic barriers, the global elite will argue that a global economy must be managed by a global government.*"[89]

The process that is being utilized by the GE is to overturn traditional values throughout global society, but especially in the United States. Once that can be accomplished, it will be much easier to change or even fully eliminate the US Constitution.

---

[86] http://www.henrymakow.com/attali.html (4/08/2014)
[87] http://www.newswithviews.com/Cuddy/dennis217.htm (4/08/2014)
[88] http://www.newswithviews.com/Cuddy/dennis223.htm (4/08/2014)
[89] Ibid.

For instance, Attali speaks of the fact that in years to come, society will have been brought to a point where monogamy is not only unexpected, but almost literally frowned upon. The GE does not want people to be in loving, life-long relationships having children who are loved. This is something that they themselves do not experience (most marriages of the GE are arranged marriages to keep wealth and bloodlines intact).

The GE wants society to become self-absorbed so that relationships do not involve reproduction. *"The elite goal is to remove love from sex so that they control reproduction. Attali writes that in the twentieth century, society 'sought to evacuate the reproductive role of sexuality by making motherhood artificial, by using increasingly sophisticated methods- pills, pre-mature labor, in vitro fertilization, surrogate mothers'."*[90]

By the way, with respect to the gay movement and their pressure to gain so-called "equality" in same-sex marriages: this is only being used now as a ruse. I don't believe many in the gay movement are even aware of it. As one gay activist has stated, *"The institution of marriage is going to change, and it should change. And again, I don't think it should exist. And I don't like taking part in creating fictions about my life. That's sort of not what I had in mind when I came out thirty years ago."*[91]

These thoughts – by Masha Gessen – provide a link to a possible underlying goal by hardcore gay activists. This is the belief that marriage should not exist at all and the first step in getting there is to overthrow marriage in terms of what it has always traditionally been about: one man and one woman joining together in holy matrimony until death do they part.

---

[90] http://www.henrymakow.com/attali.html (4/08/2014)
[91] http://www.lifesitenews.com/news/homosexual-activist-says-gay-marriage-isnt-about-equality-its-about-destroy/ (4/08/2014)

No other society has recognized same-sex unions, but today, the mad push is on by gay activists to make it so. Once this is accomplished, the traditional view of marriage will be overturned. From that point, will marriage even need to be recognized? Knowing what the GE think about marriage and their desire to control population throughout the world, it's a sure bet that they see no reason for the traditional concept of marriage to remain undamaged.

According to Attali, the world will witness a *super-empire*, followed by *hyperconflict*, which will be followed by *hyperdemocracy*. That's the way the GE have done things, in stages, bits and pieces, as they've formed one group (like the EU) or another group. It all leads to fulfilled dreams that clearly place them at the top of the heap, calling all the shots publicly, instead of as they do now, from the shadows.

In the end, the United States will most likely become a shadow of its former power. The dollar will eventually crumble completely and will be replaced with some other reserve currency (or several). A new world currency will be introduced and America will be merely one of many individual nations that wind up being dependent upon the coming "core" government.

Ultimately, human beings will exist for the pleasure of the GE. Children will be "birthed" and "grown" in laboratories, for commercial use by the GE. Remember, their goal of a one-world company in which this company is not inhibited by national boundaries, taxes, or tariffs will come to fruition, according to Attali. Once achieved, the only real purpose for human beings not part of the GE is continued use in the global empire that the GE has created.

God's stated purposes for mankind are far different from those of the GE. While He wants only the best for us – *individually* – and has provided salvation for individuals so that we can enter into a unique and individual relationship with Him, the dreams of the GE are far different.

The GE wants to use mankind for its "higher" purposes. Of course, those purposes are only to benefit them, as they believe themselves to be little gods given charge to care for this earth, to subdue and use all resources – human, animal, and natural – to make their lives the best they can possibly be. If, in the process, millions of human beings are killed (through wars, pestilence, natural disasters, etc.), so be it. The game must be played to the end. Their purposes must see the fruit of their work.

For people who are unable to see in these two extremes the difference between God and Satan, it is due to spiritual blindness. While the GE literally worships the Creation as the highest form (Gaia) and something to be protected, this same GE has upturned God's own plan so that man – the pinnacle of His Creation – is placed on the bottom. This is satanic in origin because of Satan's own jealousy toward man.

After all, God breathed into man and man became a living soul (Genesis 1-2). Satan, on the other hand, was merely created, and though he was the highest of all the creatures at that time, he was not made in God's image, as was man. Jealousy? Of course.

For this reason, Satan has determined since before the fall to use mankind as his servant to try to become what he will never be – God. In the process, he has designed to destroy humanity because it is the closest thing to God Himself. Satan has unmercifully attacked God via humanity because Satan can do nothing to God Himself.

Satan attacks man because of the fact that man was created in God's image, and it was in that image that man was given charge over all Creation, to subdue all things and rule over them.

What Satan has attempted to accomplish is what the GE believes is their intended purpose. Satan has blinded the GE to make them believe that they were put here on this earth to rule. In reality, it is Satan who yearns desperately to rule the earth and everyone on it.

This is why we have Scripture telling us that once the world's ten "kings" take their place to rule, an eleventh – a little horn – will rise up among them, kill three, and gain the loyalty of the remaining seven. He will then become the eighth (Revelation 13 and 17).

Satan is leading human beings who are thoroughly blinded to his ultimate purpose down a primrose path toward what they believe is a global empire they will rule. In reality, they have done all the groundwork and the footwork, expended the energy, and lived lives of corruption and lies in order to make it happen. They have been empowered by Satan himself.

But there is one coming who will be so given to Satan that there will be virtually no difference in the way each thinks. He will be a man who will sell himself to Satan in return for all the kingdoms of the world, all of Satan's power, and all of his authority. Through this man – the Antichrist – the global empire will be led.

But even there, though the Global Elite (GE) believes the ultimate goal is a one-world company, conveniently protected by a one-world government, Satan's true goal goes beyond that end. For the GE, it stops there, but for Satan, it actually begins there.

Satan will seek to overthrow God Himself in the form of Jesus as He returns to this planet to claim what He gained (Revelation 5). He will rule from His earthly father David's throne from Jerusalem during the Millennial Reign and He will rule with a rod of iron.

This is what the GE has no knowledge of due to their blindness. Satan knows all too well about this coming event and actually believes he can stop it.

Satan has been using the GE for centuries to insert himself into the position of power throughout the world. He cares nothing for anything God has made, especially man. His only desire s seen in gathering all the resources of the earth (including mankind's armies) for the purpose of defeating the returning, victorious King of kings and Lord of lords, Jesus.

The GE has no real clue. Believing they will live happily ever after once their goals are achieved, the truth of the matter is that it will be then that Satan will physically take over through his spiritual son, Antichrist.

Once Satan takes over, the GE may begin to wake up to the reality that they've been used. How terrible for them it will be in that day. They will come to know what terror means.

In the end, God's purposes will be fully accomplished. Victory is already His. Nothing stands in His way, not you, not me, not the GE, and not Satan. God is victor – Amen!

Chapter 17
The Elite's Future Demise

I would be completely remiss if I ended this book without offering at least some kind of solution to the problems we face in this world. If you're *not* a Christian, then the solution I'm pointing out is outlined in the next chapter, which is also the final chapter of this book.

It has come to be the way I end all of my books. There is no more important decision each person can or will make than whether or not to receive the only true salvation that is available, the very salvation that Jesus Christ made possible for us. If you do not know Jesus, then please, I cannot urge you strongly enough, receive His salvation and enter into a life-changing relationship with Him. It means the difference between heaven and hell.

However, if you *are* an authentic Christian, then this chapter will hopefully end on a high note for you. What do we do as authentic Christians who are bound to face increasing erosion of our rights under the US Constitution and greater tyranny from our own government?

There really is only one answer of which I am aware. It is twofold in nature, but it is the answer that the Bible repeatedly gives us as the means to peace in our daily walk with God.

- *Submit to His will in all things*
- *Praise Him in the midst of all things*

Honestly, is there anything else a Christian *can* or *should* do? If we believe that God controls all outcomes and that everything that comes our way will eventually work out according to His will for our good and His glory, how can we *not* submit ourselves to Him and praise Him for all things?

Difficulties of Life

I will admit that this is very difficult for me. In essence, it is the very substance of what being a Christian means. I like being in control as much as possible. When I consider what is ahead of us, I *do* become somewhat nervous and apprehensive. Will the government be able to successfully remove our guns from society? If so, what will that mean for me and my ability to protect my family from home invasions, for instance?

Is the Lord protecting me anyway? If so, should I not be casting all my cares on Him because He cares for me? That's what Peter tells us in 1 Peter 5:7. But then Paul tells us that the man who does not care for his own household is worse than an infidel (cf. 1 Timothy 5:8). That means quite a bit in reality, from things like providing food and a roof overhead to issues that revolve around safety. What do I do? How about if work becomes so difficult that we lose our jobs?

All of these things and more are the things that concern me. Some would say I'm borrowing trouble that may never come. Others would say that I should not be concerned about those things *until* they come.

The truth is that we live in a world that is constantly changing and becoming even more evil. We have talked about these things throughout these pages. Yet, in spite of everything, God is fully in control of all outcomes. If we are His – as the Bible assures us we are through faith in the finished work of Christ – then will He not provide? Will He not take care of us?

Can We Trust God or Not?
The only and obvious answer is that He *will*. In the here and now, I can and should *prepare* for coming hardships. I should do what I can to have things in my pantry and storehouse that will keep us going for up to three months – more if I can swing it. It is important that each person do what he or she can in order to *not* have to depend upon the government or others when the bottom falls out.

At the same time, we make these preparations knowing that God watches over us and cares for us. We do not know what will happen tomorrow. We do not know how far into the future total financial collapse may be. We do not know when the Rapture will occur, nor do we know when the Tribulation will begin.

Until these things occur, we also do not know how bad things will become for the average person, do we? There really is no way to know.

I believe there are many portions of Scripture that speak to the need to trust Him and let Him deal with the problems that He allows to come into our lives. Let me close this chapter by focusing on wisdom from one of the Psalms. Memorize this. Take it with you in your heart wherever you go. Learn to let it speak to you as you contemplate the problems that face your life.

The only solution to any problem we face is *God*. The only solution to any nervousness, fear, or trepidation we experience is *God*. The only solution for whatever comes into our life that brings with it sorrow, tragedy, or abysmal problems is with God. He and He alone is the answer.

It is up to us to submit these problems and difficulties to Him until we can freely and completely release them into His care. That is a must, and it truly separates those who merely say they are Christians from those who actually are Christians.

Psalm 100

Shout joyfully to the Lord, all the earth.

Serve the Lord with gladness;

Come before Him with joyful singing.

Know that the Lord Himself is God;

It is He who has made us, and not we ourselves;

We are His people and the sheep of His pasture.

Enter His gates with thanksgiving

And His courts with praise.

Give thanks to Him, bless His name.

For the Lord is good;

His lovingkindness is everlasting

And His faithfulness to all generations.

This is what we are to do. We are to first of all *shout,* and we are to shout with joy *to* the Lord. The Psalmist is literally commanding everything on the earth to call out to God with *praise*. That should be our first and continuous order of business.

Paul emphasizes this as well when he says that we should praise God in *all* things (cf. 1 Thessalonians 5:18). In doing so, we are recognizing that God is *in charge* of our lives.

But some might say, *"That is very difficult to believe!"* Yes, I know it is, but because we have a challenging time believing in something does not mean that we give up trying to believe it. It means that we have to persevere that much more until that fear turns to belief and belief turns to knowledge.

We should praise God in all things. Difficult, but it must be done if we are to exercise faith in God and His control over our lives.

Next, we should *serve* the Lord, and we should do this how? We should serve Him with *gladness*. That again is often very difficult, but there is only one solution to our doubts: *perseverance*. We cannot give up here. We must continuously praise God with everything that is within us so that we will find ourselves emotionally removed from the circumstances that wish to bind us in fear.

The Psalmist then goes on to say that our lives should be filled with joyful singing and we should come to recognize that God is our *Lord*. He is our Shepherd, and like the loving and careful shepherd who takes care of *all* the sheep in His care, God will surely do the same thing with us.

Since we are the sheep of *His* pasture, it is logical then to assume that He is the One who provides for us. His eye is always on us, our troubles, and our lives in general. He does not forget us and is always mindful of our frailties.

The Psalmist then reminds us that God is *good*. He is far more than good, but this one word helps us understand that *because* of the fact that He is good, He will do what is best for us. He is not some evil being bent on teasing us unmercifully until we bend to His deceitful will!

God has only our best interests in His heart and seeks to bring those to fruition every day. The Psalmist ends with two declarations. God's lovingkindness will never fail because it is eternal, and He is faithful to authentic Christians in *every* generation. These are two truths upon which Christians stand. We must never forget them. We must always be aware of them and we must allow these truths to penetrate our hearts and lives in order that He will be glorified in and through us.

God is not going to leave us, and when we are tempted to think that He has or will, we need to remind ourselves of the truth of Scripture. Romans 8 tells us He will never leave or forsake us and that because we are in Christ, not only are we not on the receiving end of God's condemnation, but we will *never* be on the receiving end of it!

God is good. His goodness lasts forever and it is always directed toward those who are part of His family – those who are in relationship to Jesus Christ.

The only solution that I am aware of related to the problems this life throws at us is found in submitting our will to God and praising Him in all things. Try as I might, I have found no other Scriptural remedy for life's problems, and even though I do not live these things perfectly, God always brings me back to them.

My prayer for you is that He will do the same thing for you so that your life will be filled with His peace, you will learn to trust Him in all things, and you will be freed to fulfill the Great Commission. May He be praised forever.

Chapter 18
Can Your Belief System Save You?

Do you know *when* you will die? Are you aware of the *day* and *hour* when you will slip from this life into eternity? I'm betting you are not privy to that information. So why are you living as if you **do** know when it will happen? Putting a decision about Jesus off until another day is taking a huge chance because of the fact that you do not know when you will die. That is plainly simple, and logic alone demands that you do not put this decision off. Yet you do, because the thought of becoming a Christian makes you feel uncomfortable.

You wrongly believe that to become a Christian means that you have to change in a major way *before* Jesus will accept you. It means to you giving up the things you love now because if you love them, then obviously they are wrong and God does not love them.

You are putting the cart before the horse. You must understand that God is not rejecting you. He is not standing there, tapping His foot, demanding that you eliminate those things that He does not like before you can come to Him for salvation.

If you (or anyone) could do that, you would not *need* His salvation at all. It is because you and I do things that are not pleasing to Him that we need His salvation.

What do you do that you would like to no longer do? Do you drink excessively until you cannot control it? Do you play around with drugs? Do you eat too much food until you become overweight, lethargic and sickly?

What other things are in your life that you do not like? Are you drawn to illicit extra-marital affairs? Do you have a problem with lust? Are you a shopaholic? Do you tend to tell lies a great deal because it makes you feel important, or to hide things about your life?

Do you find that you do not like people and you would prefer to be around animals or out in the woods than around people? Are you a workaholic? Do you place a high value on money and you find that you work very hard to obtain it?

Here's the problem. The enemy of our souls comes to us and tells us that God will never accept us until we get rid of those things. He lies to us that God essentially wants us "perfect" before He will be willing to meet us and grant us eternal life. This is completely untrue.

The other lie that our enemy tells us is that we should not become a Christian because the fun in our life will fly out the door. We will no longer be able to drink or do the fun things we enjoy now. We start to think that coming to God means becoming a doormat for people and having to fill our life with things we do not want to *ever* do.

These are all lies, and unfortunately, too many people believe them. First of all, God does not expect you to be "perfect" before you come to Him for salvation. If that were the case, no one would be able to ever approach Him.

Secondly, God does not say that He is going to take away all the things we enjoy and replace them with things we hate. What is wrong with enjoying the lake on your boat? What is wrong with spending a day with the family fishing or just relaxing in the mountains? There is nothing wrong with these things.

What God *will* do is begin to remove the things that have ensnared you so that life is actually draining from you, but you are not aware of it. For instance, maybe you drink excessively and you have tried everything you can think of to quit. You have gone to AA meetings, spent thousands of dollars on this program or that, and you have even used your own willpower to free yourself from the addiction to alcohol, all to no avail.

The question is not: *do I need to quit before I come to Jesus*? The question is: *am I willing to allow Him to work in and through me to take away the addiction I have to alcohol*? Do you see the difference? Are you willing to allow Him to work in you to break that addiction so that you will become a healthier person, one who is able to think straight and one who learns to rely on Him for strength? That is all He wants you to be able to do. He knows you cannot break that addiction (or any addiction for that matter) with your own strength and willpower. Are you willing to allow Him to do it in and through you?

What if you are a workaholic? What if you have "things" like a boat, a house in Cancun, a large bank account, four cars, and more? Do you think that God is going to ask you to give them up, or worse, do you think that God will simply come in and take all of that from you? I know of nothing in Scripture that tells us He will do that.

What God will do with all of those who come to Him trusting Him for salvation is one thing, which begins the moment we receive salvation and will continue until the day we stand before Him. He will begin to create within us the character of Jesus (cf. Ephesians 2:10).

Here is a verse from the Old Testament that was originally said through the prophet Ezekiel to the people of Israel. While this was specifically stated to the Jews, it is applicable to all who receive salvation through Jesus Christ.

> *I will give you a new heart and put a new spirit within you; I will take the heart of stone out of your flesh and give you a heart of flesh. I will put My Spirit within you and cause you to walk in My statutes, and you will keep My judgments and do them.* (Ezekiel 36:26-27)

God is speaking here through Ezekiel, and He is saying that He will give the people a new heart of flesh, removing that old heart of stone. This is God's responsibility. God is the One who makes that happen. We are told in the book of Hebrews that God is the Author and Finisher of our faith (cf. Hebrews 12:2). This tells me that God is the One who changes me from within so that over time, my desires are slowly turned into His desires.

I recall years ago thinking that God wanted to do everything in my life that I did not want Him to do. I fell into the asinine belief that He wanted to change everything about me. What I learned is that yes, there are things that God does want to change about me. However, there is a lot that God originally gave me that He has also enhanced and used for His glory.

Maybe you are a workaholic who thinks that working hard is something God does not want you to do. This is not necessarily the case. He may have given you the ability and the knowledge to work in the area of finance for a great purpose. All He may wind up doing is dialing back your workaholic tendencies so that you have more time to enjoy your family and study His Word.

But you say you smoke, or drink, or use illegal drugs, and you don't want to give those up. As I stated, you can't give those up under your own power, and the fact that you have tried so many times has proven it to you.

But God knows what is and what is not good for you. Are you willing to *allow* Him to work in you to change your desires so that you no longer want to smoke, use illegal drugs, or drink nearly as much?

Then you say that you believe God wants to make you a Christian so you can become miserable. Isn't that what most Christians are – miserable? Not the Christians I know, and certainly not me, my wife, or our children.

Where does the Bible say that God wants us miserable? You will not find it. What God wants is for us to be blessed, and that begins when we receive salvation from His hand.

You know, if we stop and take the time to consider the fact that this life is exceedingly short if we compare it to eternity, we will then realize that there is nothing so important that it should keep us from receiving Jesus as Savior and Lord.

Unfortunately, too many people do not consider the brevity of life. They think they will live forever, or at the very least, they will die when they are really old and gray. That will come too soon. Even though I have just recently turned 57, it still truly seems like yesterday that I was a young boy fishing in the Delaware River near Hobart, New York. There I spent many Saturdays fishing and simply enjoying being outdoors. How did life go by so very quickly? How could that have happened?

It has happened, and I am at a point in life where not only do I realize that this life is short, but I actually look forward to spending eternity with Jesus after this life. Does that sound morbid to you? It shouldn't, because by comparing this life to eternity, we should get a sense of what is truly important.

God does not expect us to become Mother Theresas. He does not necessarily expect us to give up everything and become missionaries in outer Mongolia. What God expects is for us to simply allow Him to change our character as He sees fit.

Over time, we may well find that we have simply stopped swearing without realizing it. Our desire for cigarettes or alcohol has nearly evaporated. Illicit affairs no longer enter the picture.

We also may find that some of the things we want to eliminate in our life become more pronounced. Often the enemy will do this to cause us to focus on something that God is not even doing in our lives at that point. It causes tension, frustration, and self-anger.

If you have gotten to this point in your life and you have not dealt with the question about Jesus, it is about time you do so. You need to stop what you are doing and realize a couple of things before you go through another minute in this life.

- **Sinner**: you need to realize that you are a sinner. You have sinned and you will continue to sin. Sin is breaking the laws that God has set up. We all sin. We have all broken God's laws and that breaks any connection we might have had with God. Sin pushes us away from Him.

  Romans 3:23 says, *"For all have sinned, and come short of the glory of God."* That means you and that means me. All means all. That is the first step. We need to recognize and agree with God that yes, we are sinners. I'm a sinner. You are a sinner. This results in God's anger, what the Bible terms "wrath."

- **God's Wrath**: Romans 1:18 says, *"For the wrath of God is revealed from heaven against all ungodliness and unrighteousness of men, who suppress the truth in unrighteousness."*

This is as much a fact as the truth that we are all sinners. Because we are sinners – by breaking God's law(s) – God has every right to be angry with us and ultimately destroy that which is sinful. If we choose to remain "in" our sinful states throughout this life, we will – unfortunately – be destroyed with the rest of sin.

Fortunately, there *is* a remedy, and it is salvation.

- **God's Gift**: In the sixteenth chapter of Acts, a jailer asks Paul this famous question: *what must I do to be saved?* The question was asked because Paul and Barnabas had been imprisoned, and while there, they began singing praises to God.

God then sent a powerful earthquake that opened the doors to all the prison cells, yet no one escaped. When the jailer arrived, he saw that everyone was still in their cells, and after seeing that miracle (what prisoner would not want to escape from prison?), turned and asked what he must do to be saved. He was speaking of the spiritual aspect of things. He wanted to know how he could be guaranteed eternal life.

The answer Paul gave the man was, *"Believe on the Lord Jesus Christ, and thou shalt be saved, and thy house"* (Acts 16:31).

This is not head knowledge or intellectual assent. This is *believing from the heart.* In fact, Paul makes a very similar statement in another book he wrote, Romans. He says, *"That if thou shalt confess with thy mouth the Lord Jesus, and shalt believe in thine heart that God hath raised him from the dead, thou shalt be saved. For with the heart man believeth unto righteousness; and with the mouth confession is made unto salvation"* (Romans 10:9-10).

When we fully believe something, we confess that it is true. It must begin in the heart because that is where the will is located. We must want to believe. We must endeavor to believe. We must seek to believe.

We must stop giving ourselves all the reasons to deny or ignore Jesus. As God, He became a Man, born of a virgin. He clothed Himself with humanity that He might show us how to live, and in so doing, would keep every portion of the law.

If Jesus was capable of keeping every portion of the law, then He would be found worthy to become a sacrifice for our sin – yours and mine. If He became a sacrifice for our sin, then all that we must do is embrace Him and His sacrificial death.

In short then, to become saved we must:

1. Admit (we sin)
2. Repent (want to turn away from it)
3. Believe (that Jesus is the answer)
4. Embrace (the truth about Jesus)

We **admit** that we are sinner, that we have sinned. This is nothing more than agreeing with God that we have broken His law. Can you honestly say that you have not broken God's law? If you admit to breaking even the "smallest" law, then you are a lawbreaker.

After we admit that we have sinned, the next step is found in **repenting**. Some believe that repenting is actually moving away from sin. This author believes that it is a willingness to move away from sin, and there is a difference.

As we have already discussed, it is impossible to stop sinning. Human beings simply cannot do it because as long as we live, we will have a sin nature, which is something within us that gives us a propensity to sin. As long as we have this inner propensity to sin or break God's laws, we will never be perfect in this life.

We cannot one day say, "Lord, I promise to stop sinning." If we do that, we are only kidding ourselves and setting ourselves up for major failure. We cannot stop sinning in this life. The most we can do is *want* to stop sinning and then spend the rest of our lives allowing God to create the character of Jesus within us, slowly, little by little.

Repenting is to decide that you no longer want to do the things that keep us out of heaven. We no longer wish to break God's laws. It is not promising God that we will never sin again.

Once we admit, then repent, we must **believe**. This is one of the most difficult things to do because believing that Jesus died in our place, that He lived a perfectly sinless life, is extremely difficult. Our minds cannot grasp that truth. We must ask God to open our eyes to that truth so that we can embrace it.

While on the cross next to Jesus, the one thief joined the other thief in ridiculing Jesus. Then, all of a sudden – as we read in Luke 23 – this same thief that had just been ridiculing Him now turned to Him with a new understanding.

It was this new understanding that prompted the thief to say to Jesus, *"Lord, remember me when you come into your Kingdom."* Jesus looked at the man and responded to him, *"Today, you will be with me in paradise."*

What had occurred in the mind and heart of that thief from one moment to the next? One thing, and that one thing was that God opened the thief's eyes so that he could see the truth. It was as if the blinders fell off and he now saw and understood who Jesus was, even to the most cursory degree that Jesus was dying not for Himself, but for others.

It was this understanding, this awareness, which prompted the man to ask Jesus to simply be remembered. Jesus went way beyond it to promise the man that he would be with Jesus that day in paradise.

Please notice in Luke 23 that there is nothing in the chapter that tells us that the man promised Jesus he would give up sin, or that he would never sin again. There is nothing that tells us that thief took the time to enter into a final deathbed confession of his sins so that he could be absolved.

The thief made no promises to Jesus at all. What he experienced was the truth of who Jesus was and what Jesus accomplished for humanity. Jesus accomplished what we cannot. What is left is for each person to *admit, repent, believe,* and *embrace*.

Let me clarify here that though we do not see any verbal repentance from the thief, we know that he did repent. He admitted as well. How can we know this? It is simply due to the thief's complete about-face with respect to his attitude toward Jesus. One minute, he was ridiculing Jesus, and the next, embracing Him. This is important. There is no way he could have or would have *embraced* Jesus had he not been humbled by the truth *about* Jesus.

Once the thief saw the truth, he was instantly humbled. Within himself, he knew that he was a sinner, and in fact the text states that this is what he told the other thief dying next to him. *"But the other answering rebuked him, saying, Dost not thou fear God, seeing thou art in the same condemnation? And we indeed justly; for we receive the due reward of our deeds: but this man hath done nothing amiss"* (Luke 23:40-41). Something happened within the heart of the one thief. In one moment, the thief went from harassing Jesus to recognizing his own sinfulness and then ultimately asking for grace, which was freely given to him.

Whether he said it or not, the thief went from haughtiness to humility in a very short space of time, and it was all because he saw the truth about Jesus. That truth helped him realize that he deserved his death and what would happen to him after death. He understood that Jesus did not deserve death.

From here, the thief fully embraced the truth about Jesus and was rewarded with eternal life because of it. He did not come off the cross to be water baptized. He did not list a long litany of offenses against God. He recognized the truth about Jesus, was humbled, and embraced that truth!

This is what each of us needs to do. We cannot give in to the lie that tells us that we are not good enough, or we have not given up enough before God will accept us. We must reject the lie that says we must somehow earn our salvation.

Jesus has done everything that is necessary to make salvation available to us. The only thing that is left for us is to see the truth. Once we see that truth, it should humble us to the point of embracing Jesus and all that He stands for and is to us.

The eighth chapter of Romans begins with the fact that all who trust Jesus for salvation are no longer condemned...*ever*. All of my sins – past, present, and future – have not only been forgiven, but canceled. It is because of my faith in the atonement (death) of Jesus that God is able to cancel all of my sins, even the ones that I have not committed yet. This does not make me eager to commit them. It makes me want to do what I can to avoid sinning.

If you do not know Jesus, please do not put down this book without deliberately *believing* that He is God, that He died for you by the shedding of His blood on the cross, and that He rose three days later because death could not keep Him. Do you believe that? If you do not yet believe it, do you *want* to believe it? If so, then simply ask God to help you come to believe all that Jesus is and all that He has accomplished for you. God will answer your prayers and you may either receive instantaneous awareness of all that Jesus is and has done, or it may be a *growing* awareness over time. In either case, it is the most important decision you will ever make.

Turn to Him now and pray for knowledge of the truth and an ability to embrace it. Please. He is waiting for you.

Ask Yourself:

1. Do you *know* Jesus? Are you in *relationship* with Him? Have you had a spiritual transaction according to John 3?
2. Do you *want* to receive eternal life through the only salvation that is available?
3. Do you believe that Jesus is God the Son, who was born of a virgin, lived a sinless life, died a bloody and gruesome death to pay for your sin, was buried, and rose again on the third day? Do you *believe* this?
4. Do you *want* to *embrace* the truth from #3?
5. Pray that God will open your eyes and provide you with the faith to begin believing the truth about Jesus. Ask Him to help your faith embrace the truth, realizing that you are not good enough to save yourself and that your sin will keep you out of God's Kingdom without His salvation.
6. Pray as if your life depended upon it because *it does*!
7. If you have prayed to receive Jesus as Savior and Lord, please write to me. I want to send you some materials at *no charge or obligation*. Write to me at **fred_deruvo@hotmail.com** and sign up for our free bimonthly newsletter at **www.studygrowknow.com**

Resources for Your Library

- *A Brief History of the Future*, Jacques Attali
- *A Government of Wolves*, John W. Whitehead
- *America's Nazi Secret*, John Loftus
- *America's Secret Establishment*, Antony C. Sutton
- *Atlas of World History*, Edited by Kate Santon/Liz McKay
- *Behold a Pale Horse*, William Cooper
- "Brief Guide to Al-Haram Al-Sharif Jerusalem" (Supreme Muslim Council, 1924)
- *Caught in the Grip of Political Correctness*, Fred DeRuvo
- *Conspirator's Hierarchy*, Dr. John Coleman
- *Diplomacy by Deception*, Dr. John Coleman
- *Dismantling America*, Thomas Sowell
- *Falling Away*, Fred DeRuvo
- *Family of Secrets*, Russ Baker
- *Fast Facts on Islam*, John Ankerberg/John Weldon
- *Frenzied Finance*, Thomas W. Lawson
- *Friendly Fascism*, Bertram Gross
- *History of Rome*, Michael Grant
- "Introduction to Islam," Zahid Aziz
- *Islam and the Muslim World*, Mir Zohair Husain
- *Islam: In Light of History*, Dr. Rafat Amari
- *Living in the Last Generation*, Fred DeRuvo
- *Memoirs*, David Rockefeller
- *Mental Health, Education, and Social Control*, Dennis L. Cuddy
- *New World Order: The Rise of Techno-Feudalism*, Dennis L. Cuddy
- "Notes on Daniel," Dr. Thomas Constable
- "Notes on Revelation," Dr. Thomas Constable
- *One Nation, Under Attack*, Grant R. Jeffrey
- *Plundered: How Progressive Ideology is Destroying America*, Michael S. Coffman

- *Proofs of a Conspiracy*, John Robison
- *Propaganda*, Edward Bernays
- *Relativism: Feet Firmly Planted in Mid-Air*, Francis J. Beckwith/Gregory Koukl
- *Rule by Secrecy*, Jim Marrs
- *SCAM: How the Black Leadership Exploits Black America*, Rev. Jesse Lee Peterson
- *Secret Lives of the US Presidents*, by Cormac O'Brien
- *Shadow Government*, Grant R. Jeffrey
- *Shadow Masters*, Daniel Estulin
- *Strategic Vision*, Zbigniew Brzezinski
- *The American Axis*, Max Wallace
- *The True Story of the Bilderberg Group*, Daniel Estulin
- "The Club of Rome," by Dr. John Coleman
- "The Committee of 300," Dr. John Coleman
- *The Complete Idiot's Guide to World History*, Timothy C. Hall
- *The Complete Infidel's Guide to the Koran*, Robert Spencer
- *The Illuminati: Facts & Fiction*, Mark Dice
- *The Illuminati in America*, Dr. John Coleman
- *The Inheritance of Rome*, Chris Wickham
- *The Most Dangerous Book in the World: 9/11 as Mass Ritual*, S. K. Bain
- *The Nazi Connection to Islamic Terrorism*, Chuck Morse
- *The Open Conspiracy*, H. G. Wells
- *The Ottoman Empire 1700 – 1922*, Donald Quataert
- *The Politically Incorrect Guide to Islam*, Robert Spencer
- *The Power Elite and the Secret Nazi Plan*, Dennis L. Cuddy
- *The Power Elite*, Dennis L. Cuddy
- *The Retreat of Reason*, Anthony Browne
- *The Road to Socialism and the New World Order*, Dennis L. Cuddy
- *The Roots of Nazi Psychology : Hitler's Utopian Barbarism*, Jay Y. Gonen

- *The Secret Destiny of America*, Manly P. Hall
- *The Secret Teachings of All Ages*, Manly P. Hall
- *The Tavistock Institute of Human Relations: Shaping the Moral, Spiritual, Cultural, and Political*, Dr. John Coleman
- *The Truth About Islam*, Lon Roberts

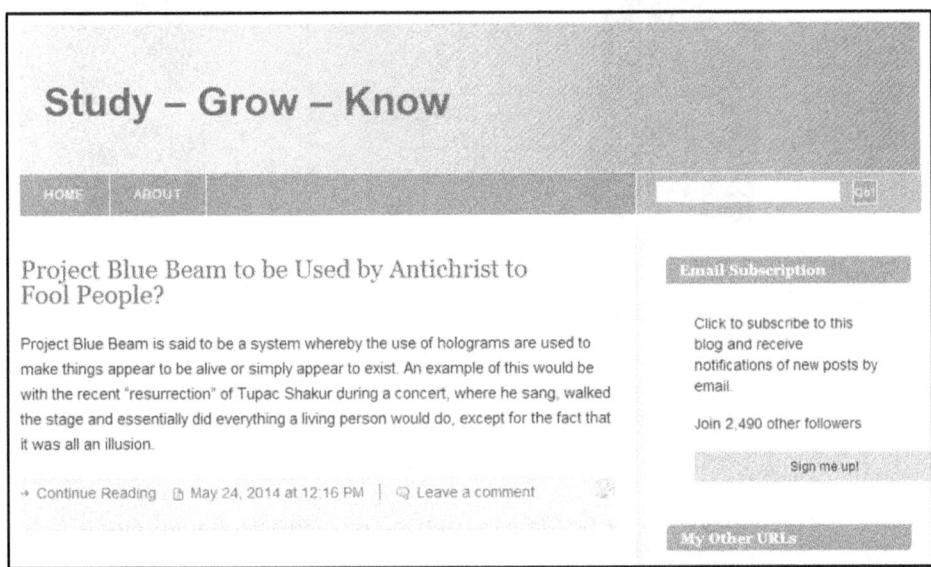

Keep tabs on www.studygrowknowblog.com (top) and our messages at www.sermonaudio.com/studygrowknow (bottom)

Rome Rising

Stop by our Internet page…http://studygrowknow.com

And check out our books to purchase or…**FREE** to download.

www.ingramcontent.com/pod-product-compliance
Lightning Source LLC
LaVergne TN
LVHW061217060426
835508LV00014B/1337